THE JUDGMENT OF A CATHOLICKE ENGLISH-MAN
LIVING IN BANISHMENT FOR HIS RELIGION

THE
JUDGMENT

OF A CATHOLICKE ENGLISH-MAN

LIVING IN BANISHMENT FOR HIS RELIGION
(1608)

BY

ROBERT PERSONS

A FACSIMILE REPRODUCTION

WITH AN INTRODUCTION

BY

WILLIAM T. COSTELLO, S.J.
Gonzaga University

GAINESVILLE, FLORIDA

SCHOLARS' FACSIMILES & REPRINTS

1957

SCHOLARS' FACSIMILES & REPRINTS
118 N.W. 26TH STREET
GAINESVILLE, FLORIDA
HARRY R. WARFEL, GENERAL EDITOR

REPRODUCED FROM A COPY IN
AND WITH THE PERMISSION OF

CROSBY MEMORIAL LIBRARY

OF

GONZAGA UNIVERSITY

L.C. CATALOG CARD NUMBER 57-9033

MANUFACTURED IN THE U.S.A.
LETTERPRESS BY WAYSIDE PRESS
PHOTOLITHOGRAPHY BY EDWARDS BROTHERS
BINDING BY UNIVERSAL-DIXIE BINDERY

INTRODUCTION

Robert Persons, S.J. (sometimes mis-spelled "Parsons") is supposed to be the intaglio for the Jesuit of fiction. But the Father Holts and Pére Rodins, who intrigue always in the dark of the moon, laying plots and inductions dangerous, burning papers at midnight and disappearing into the woodwork, are only murky and unbelievable counterfeits of one of the most fascinating personalities of Elizabethan-Jacobean England. Like Sidney and Raleigh, Persons was involved in high exploit and lofty enterprise; like Jonson and Donne, he was capable of warm friendship and the object of fierce loyalty. He could write popular prose with Nashe and Greene, and still be ranked with Richard Hooker as a serious stylist by no less an authority than Jonathan Swift (*Tatler,* 230). Vilified by James I, Edward Coke, Francis Hastings, William Watson, and a baker's dozen other adversaries, he was the beloved confidant of Edmund Campion, Robert Southwell, and Cardinal Allen, whose virtue and intelligence are beyond cavil. The activities in which Persons, Campion, and their fellow Jesuits engaged for the reconversion of England have been censured by hostile critics as wrongheaded, divisive, traitorous, imprudent, even disobedient, but no serious modern historian challenges Persons' intellectual and moral integrity, his courage, or his devotion to an unselfish ideal.

Persons' courage and resourcefulness are legendary. No Jesuit of fiction can match the derring-do, whereby, with the Channel ports closed specifically against him and with pursuivants swarming, Persons re-entered England in 1580. Outfitted by a Mr. Chamberlain, an English Catholic serving in the Spanish forces, in "a very fit suit of captain's apparel . . . which was of buff laid with gold and with hat and feather suited to the same," Persons disembarked at Dover on the morning of June 16, 1580, and so successfully played his part as a swaggering captain in his borrowed finery that the searcher commissioned to examine him "found no cause of doubt in him, but let him pass with all favour, procuring him both horse and all things necessary for his journey to Gravesend" (Persons' *Life of Campion*, c. 18; cited in Leo Hicks, S.J., *Letters and Memorials of Father Robert Persons, S.J.* [1942], I, p. xv). In a parting act of effrontery, Persons told the port-inspector that "a merchant friend of his, lying at St. Omer, of the name of Edmonds, would shortly follow him to England and asked that a like favour might be shown him" (Hicks, I, p. xv). Edmonds was, of course, Edmund Campion, who delayed his own journey long enough to describe Persons' curious getup in a letter to the Jesuit General (June 20, 1580): "He was dressed up like a soldier—such a peacock, such a swaggerer, that a man needs must have very sharp eyes to catch a glimpse of any holiness and modesty shrouded beneath such a garb, such a look, such a strut" (in Richard Simpson, *Edmund Campion, a Biography* [1866], p. 174).

Not all of Persons' exploits were thus picturesque. Born of good yeoman stock in Somerset, 1546, he found his way to Oxford, where after taking his degree he was elected fellow of Balliol. In 1575 Persons was forced to resign his fellowship because of a quarrel with the Master of Balliol, Adam Squire, who maintained that Persons "perverted a great number of students and that it was not meet for a man of his backwardness in religion to have so many pupils of quality" (Hicks, I, p. x). Whatever the real reason for the quarrel, the Master and fellows "ringing the bells of S.

Mary Magdalen's, shut him out of the College." Not yet
a papist, Persons went abroad to Louvain, where he made
the Ignatian spiritual exercises under Fr. William Good, an
English Jesuit, was converted to Roman Catholicism, proceeded to Rome, and entered the Jesuit novitiate of S.
Andrea. After his theological studies he was ordained priest,
probably in 1578, and two years later was sent with Campion
to England.

Now follow thirteen energetic months of missionary
labor in England, where Persons toured the counties, set
up the famous secret press in East Ham, and began the
long series of controversial writings which were to occupy
him between journeys, administrative duties, and countless
negotiations until his death. The exploits of Persons and
Campion, culminating in the printing of Campion's *Decem
Rationes* and the audacious distribution of the book on the
very benches at the Academical Act at Oxford in the spring
of 1581, aroused the government to feverish activity, with
the result that Campion was captured on July 17, and Persons
was forced to flee a few weeks later to France. The winter
of 1581 he spent at Rouen, writing among other things
his famous *The First Book of the Christian Exercise* (1582),
the most widely read ascetical book in England, among both
Catholics and Protestants, until Richard Baxter's *Saints'
Everlasting Rest* (1650) and Jeremy Taylor's *Holy Dying*
(1651). Protestants used mostly Edmund Bunny's pirated
version, called *A Book of Christian Exercise* (1584), which
had been safely bowdlerized of all "Catholic errors and
corruption."

In 1584 Persons was concerned with the possible escape
of Mary Stuart. On October 10 of that year, with the support of Mary's French kindred and the apparent knowledge of Philip II, Persons wrote the Queen of Scots at
Wingfeld, where she was being held.

His review of the situation and his suggestions of various methods of escape were in his typically graceful style: "But now for this manner of escape if yowr Majestye can assure us that yow can but yowr selfe with one or two persons disguised abowt midnight withowt the howse where as [*sic*] yow lye, and so provide that it may be kept secret for two or three howres after we dowt not but so to provide for the rest that all England shall never take yow agayne, whatsoever pursute may or shalbe made after yow wee shall finde I dowte not both tall and trustye fellowes both by land and sea and resolute to spend theyr lives in the service. And if yowr majestye can be browght to the sea side there shall be a vessell redye sufficientlye provided to brooke the sea from England in what way soever if God say Amen. If the thing be attempted it must nedes be in these longe winter nightes" (Hicks, I, pp. 247-248).

An historical novelist might make a good deal of such ingredients of high romance as a royal beauty in durance vile, disguises, winter midnights, and storm at sea. But the situation was far too tragically desperate for Mary and the Catholic cause to be romanticized, and sober history must relate that Persons' letter had been intercepted by the English government and held up for a year and a half. Meantime, between the dispatch of Persons' letter and its reception, Mary had been removed from Wingfeld, first to Tutbury in January, 1585, and later to the maximum security of Charteley in December of the same year. Accordingly, from Charteley, on May 28, 1586, Mary replied to Persons that, had she received his letter while still at Wingfeld, she "cold have browght that to pass which you did propone unto me. ... But now both my selfe and my folkes here are so straightly looked unto and kept so close as it hath not hithertill bene in my power to practise any within this Howse to my devotion except hym onlye that leadeth this entercowrse. And withowt I were assisted by

some of my kepars servantes it is now altogether impossible
for me to escape the gates onlye never a window in my
lodging nor way abowt the howse being almost eyther day
or night withowt a sentinell: wherfore for this desseing
[design] of my deliverye I can putt yow in no hope con-
sydring the state I am in presentlye" (Hicks, I, p. 357).

Such business was, however, the least important and
enduring of Persons' activities on behalf of the English
Catholics. From 1585 to 1588, Persons was in Rome, serving briefly as Latin secretary to the Jesuit General and later
as rector of the English College. In October of 1588, Persons was sent to Spain to discuss certain matters affecting
Spanish Jesuits which were causing difficulties with Philip
II. He used his time in Spain well, establishing the seminaries of Valladolid, Seville, and Madrid, among others.
Persons' most important foundation, however, was none
of the Spanish seminaries but the famous school for boys
at St. Omer, which Persons founded in 1593, and which
was to be for many generations the greenhouse of English
Catholicism.

Persons returned from Spain in 1597, arriving at
Rome in March. He found the English College upset by
certain "stirs" or dissensions, which had arisen largely over
the question of the English succession. He settled the stirs
finally in September, and though he thought his stay in
Rome was to be short and was anxious to get back to Spain,
he was never to do so. Appointed rector of the English
College in November, 1597, he continued in that post to
his death in 1610. Between times this "Jesuit beyonde the
seas, yet an English man," managed to write a succession of
books: *A Temperate Ward-word to ... Sir Francis Hastinges*
(1599), *A Brief Apologie* (1602), *A Manifestation of the
Great Folly* (1602). These, among others, earned him his
reputation as "the most active, the ablest, and the most in-
fluential" among the antagonists of Elizabeth (Charles H.

McIlwain, ed., *The Political Works of James I* [1918], p. 1).

Meanwhile James had succeeded to the throne and the insuperable problems of a religiously divided realm. Modern historians are rather more charitable with regard to James' intelligence than their predecessors, but even heroic charity cannot match James' capacity for recognizing his own ability, particularly in matters of pastoral theology. James, deftly managed by Robert Cecil in most matters relating to English policy, twice interposed his theological talents to his own cost. The Hampton Court Conference (1604), over which James presided in person, accomplished nothing; if anything, he alienated further the Presbyterians and Puritans by indulging his persistent delusion that all men must relish his theological haggis. In the long run, however, it was James' second incursion into theological affairs through his personal involvement in the controversy surrounding the Oath of Allegiance (1606) that ruined him as a paragon of prince-theologians.

The genesis of the Oath of Allegiance (and of Robert Persons' present volume) was basically a shrewd application of the maxim *divide et impera*. The Catholics were already split into two parties: one was under the leadership of the Jesuits, who stood for Papal supremacy in matters spiritual; the other was under the Appellants, who were a group of Anglicanizing fellow-travelers among the Catholic clergy. In an effort to exploit the rift (certainly not as a bona fide test of loyalty) Commons passed, May 27, 1606, "An Act for the Better Discovery and Repressing of Popish Recusants," enjoining an oath, which at first reading seemed to require, innocuously enough, that a Catholic "abhorre, detest, and abjure, as impious and hereticall, this damnable doctrine and position, That Princes which bee excommunicated or deprived by the Pope, may be deposed or murthered by their subjects, or any other whatsoever." Although the apparent occasion for the oath was the discovery of the Gunpowder Plot, November 5, 1605, the fact is that the oath-formulas, whose initial drafting is traceable to the Appellants, were finally drawn up early in 1605, before the Powder Plot, by Richard Bancroft, Bishop of London. It was hoped that the Jesuits would discredit themselves with the majority of the Catholic laity by opposing the oath; the Appellants would subscribe to it and thus emerge as the leaders of the "good" Catholics as against the Jesuited "bad" (See James Brodrick, S.J., *Robert Bellarmine* [1928], II, pp. 175-177).

The oath was, as Brodrick describes it, "a clever blend of perfectly legitimate declarations with highly controversial ones" (II, p. 176). It involved not only the logical fallacy of the *quaestio complexa,* whereby a Catholic must abjure as impious and heretical the damnable doctrine of regicide (which is like making a man swear that he will stop beating his wife), but further required that a Catholic forswear "as impious and hereticall" the doctrine that a king who is excommunicated or deprived by the Pope may be *deposed* by his subjects. Leaving aside the truth or falsity of the theory of the deposing power (the theory had the support of most Catholic theologians), the oath, in effect, asked a Catholic to swear that King James and Parliament were for him the final arbiters of orthodoxy, since what the Catholic theologians were teaching was described in the oath as *heretical.* By the Oath of Allegiance, as Leopold von Ranke points out, "the supremacy of the King would be practically acknowledged and the connection of the English Catholics with the Papacy dissolved" (*History of England, Principally in the* 17*th Century* [1875], I, p. 416).

Four months after the passage of the act, on September 22, 1606, Paul V signed a brief pronouncing the oath unlawful for Catholics. The aged Archpriest Blackwell, the official leader of the Catholics in England, had several times changed his position with respect to the oath; finally, after his capture, June 24, 1607, he took the oath himself and wrote a letter urging it on his flock. Blackwell's yielding called forth a second brief from the Pope, August, 1607, which reasserted the prohibition contained in the previous brief. Qn September 28, 1607, apparently at the Pope's suggestion, Cardinal Bellarmine wrote to Blackwell a frank but kindly letter, in which he chided the archpriest and insisted on the intransigency necessary with respect to the oath.

James saw in Bellarmine's letter to Blackwell a call to the lists. Against the advice of his ministers, he framed an answer to the Cardinal, issuing on February 14, 1608, the little volume, *Triplici Nodo Triplex Cuneus* (A Threefold Wedge to a Threefold Knot). While the book was officially anonymous, its authorship was an open secret, the royal arms, the style, and, above all, the contents identifying the author at once.

James' book, sub-titled *An Apologie for the Oath of Allegiance,* begins with a gracious encomium of himself as a model of benevolent kingship, particularly in view of the Powder-Treason of unhappy memory. He pays tribute to Elizabeth, "that blessed defunct LADIE," and "hauing sacrificed (if I may so say) to the *Manes* of my late Predecessour" (*The Political Works,* p. 76), he proceeds to criticize the two briefs and to attack Bellarmine. Bellarmine, he feels, is making a mountain out of a molehill, for James affects to see no question of royal supremacy involved. "For in all this Letter of his [Bellarmine's], neuer one word is vsed to prooue that by any part of this Oath the Primacie of Saint *Peter* is any way medled with, except Master *Bellarmine* his bare alleadging" (*The Political Works,* p. 91). (Persons' reply will make James rue the slighting reference here and elsewhere to *Master* Bellarmine.) In fact, says the King, the enforcement of the Oath of Allegiance should be considered by Catholics as an act of grace: "Nay, could there be a more gracious part in a King, suppose I say it, towards Subjects of a contrary Religion, then by making them to take this Oath, to publish their honest fidelitie in temporal things to their Soueraigne, and thereby to wipe off that imputation and great slander which was laide vpon the whole professours of that Religion, by the furious enterprise of these Powder-men?" (*The Political Works,* p. 97) James' graciousness, in view of the origin of the oath and the context of the staggeringly severe Penal Code which remained unaltered, is hardly to be taken seriously.

James harps upon his point that the Oath of Allegiance is not an Oath of Supremacy, but his effort is largely expended in proving learnedly from Scripture, the Fathers, and the Councils that, despite papal pronouncements and actions in the past, a king is entitled to civil obedience, a point which Persons will insist is not in contention. Whether or not "the State of the Question is twice or thrice changed in this Apologie," as Persons charges (pp. 2-3), the fact remains that James' book is solemnly erudite and often eloquent. James Brodrick pays this tribute: "Despite the unmannerly language and less than regal insinuations, the Apology was genuinely learned, and would not have been a discredit to the best scholar on the Anglican bench of Bishops" (*Robert Bellarmine,* II, p. 191).

Really at issue between James and Bellarmine was the central question of the English Reformation, royal versus papal supremacy, with the annexed question of the divine right of kings. Persons takes up both issues in his reply to the King, dividing his book into three sections or "paragraphs," which correspond roughly to the threefold division of James' book. Paragraph I is concerned with the substance of the oath and the question of papal supremacy; Paragraph II refutes James on the papal briefs; and Paragraph III, almost half of the book, defends Bellarmine.

While Persons follows James in organizing his materials, he does not imitate the King's dour solemnity. With delicious irony, using a trick which Voltaire will later employ against Maupertuis, Persons pretends that he does not recognize the author of *Triplici Nodo;* indeed, he feels that it must be the work of some inferior minister, who has usurped the King's arms and has somehow tricked the King's own printer into unauthorized publication. In fact, Persons does not think that James could even have read the book, not only because "the State of the Question is twice or thrice changed," but because no one as gracious and honorable as the King would ever refer to a Cardinal as "Master," for, "if his Ma[jes]tie had had the perusall of the *Booke,* before it came forth, he would presently haue gyuen a dash of his pen ouer it, with effectuall order to remedy such ouersightes of inciuility" (p. 4).

But Persons soon drops his gay twitting of his Majesty and begins to riposte in earnest. Does the King boast of his clemency? Why, then, "is there no end of exprobation against the Innocent for the Nocent? No compassion? No commiseration? ... How come so many searches of their houses, spoyle of their goods, apprehensions of their persons, afflictions of their tennants, seruants & friends, so many citations, attachments, vexations, and molestations, that dayly do flow vpon them, as if they were the only malefactours of the Land?" (p. 7) One must go back to Hugh Latimer, perhaps even to Wulfstan, for a more stirring example of rhetorical accumulation (*synathroesmus,* as Persons would have called it). To view the passage as mere rhetoric, however, would be to misconceive the deadly seriousness of Persons' charge.

Persons is not always so Latinate as the above passage would indicate, for, while he does savor such Latinizing as "the Innocent for the Nocent," or "compounded by artificiall ioyning together of Temporall and Spirituall" (p. 15), or "exulceration maketh them fester more greiuously" (p. 128), he is much more likely to cut his Latin syrup with an acidulous Anglo-Saxonism. His "vayne & brickle felicityes of this world" (p. 32) shines like shook foil. And who would tamper with "vnspeakable affliction and angariation of mynd" (p. 21), or "sacrificing to the *Manes* or Hob-gob-lins of his late Lady" (p. 27), or "vpon the egging of others, more then of her owne propension" (p. 33)? Persons' prose attracts the discriminating and while one might wish to temper Isaac Disraeli's enthusiasm, one must agree when he says: "Parsons may be ranked among the earliest writers of our vernacular diction, in its purity and pristine vigour, without ornament, or polish. It is, we presume, Saxon English, unblemished by an exotic phrase. It is remarkable that our author, who passed the best part of his days abroad, and who had perfectly acquired the Spanish and Italian languages, and slightly the French, yet appears to have preserved our colloquial English from the vicissitudes of those fashionable novelties which deform the long unsettled Elizabethan prose" (*Amenities of Litera-ture* [1880], II, p. 85). Persons does seem to have escaped the unhealthy vapors of Euphuism, but he Latinizes rather more than Disraeli would admit.

Be this as it may, even the most casual reader will discover a lively grassrootedness, something always a little extra, wherever he opens Persons. Perhaps it is Persons' habit of thinking in figures (he shows a rhetorician's ap-preciation for the snares of *similitudo,* pp. 106-107) that makes his prose so tangy and fermentative. He describes James' bookish industry as a bringing forth examples "with his wet finger" (p. 37). Elsewhere, "examples are heaped together to make a muster of witnesses" (p. 99). The issue is "drawne ... into the Vniuersall Theatre of the world" (p. 127).

There is something genuinely touching about the conclusion of *The Judgment of a Catholicke English-man, Living in Banishment for his Religion,* something that makes one think of the dejected Milton's plea for "the good old cause" in *The Readie & Easy Way.* Persons' love of England shines out in: "Nothing can be more pitifull, then to see a Noble House diuided in itselfe" (p. 124), and he can only conclude wisely but sadly: "I neuer heard or read, that too much violence towards free Subjects euer ended well" (p. 128).

But Persons did not have the last word. *The Judgment of a Catholicke English-man* "was too able and too important to leave unanswered in England" (McIlwain, *The Political Works,* p. lxii), and James was never one to leave a gauntlet on the ground. To a new edition (1609) of *Triplici Nodo,* James prefixed "A Premonition to All Most Mightie Monarches," in which he fairly splutters at "the English Paragraphist, or rather peruerse Pamphleter *Parsons,* since all his description must runne vpon a P." (*The Political Works,* p. 112). He is even more angry that Persons has dared challenge the Elizabeth myth, already a-building, though Persons has been hardly more than irreverently humorous (p. 27) about the "gracious defunct ladie" to whom he and his brethren owed so little. James fumes royally: "As for the English *Answere,* my vnnaturall and fugitiue Subject, I will neither defile my pen, nor your sacred eyes or eares with the describing of him, who ashames, nay, abhorres not to raile, nay, to rage and spew foorth blasphemies against the late Queene of famous memory. A Subject to raile against his naturall Soueraigne by birth; A man to raile against a Ladie by sexe; A holy man (in outward profession) to insult vpon the dead. ... Cursed be he that curseth the Anointed of God. ... Without mought such dogs and swine be cast forth, I say, out of the Spirituall Ierusalem" (*The Political Works,* p. 114).

But all the King's ranting and all the King's men cannot unsay a single word of Persons' little book. Particularly must stand what are perhaps the most important words Persons ever wrote: "at the beginning God did not immediately appoynt these particuler and different formes of Temporall gouernment, which now the world hath, but appoynted only, that there should be Gouernment, leauing to ech nation to take or choose what they would" (p. 121). Here is the English wellspring of the tradition which will run from Bellarmine-Persons, through Locke, to Jefferson, and will result in the document which states among other things that "governments· are instituted among men, deriving their just powers from the consent of the governed."

WILLIAM T. COSTELLO, S.J.

Gonzaga University

THE JUDGMENT OF A CATHOLICKE ENGLISH-MAN
LIVING IN BANISHMENT FOR HIS RELIGION

THE
IVDGMENT
OF A CATHOLICKE
ENGLISH-MAN, LIVING IN
BANISHMENT FOR HIS RELIGION:
VVritten to his priuate friend
in England.

Concerninge A late BOOKE *set forth, and entituled;*

Triplici nodo, triplex cuneus,

Or, An Apologie for the Oath of Allegiance.

Againſt two BREVES of Pope-PAVLVS V. to the Catholickes of *England*; & a Letter of Cardinall BELLARMINE
to M. GEORGE BLACKWELL Arch-prieſt.

VVherin, the ſaid Oath *is ſhewed to be vnlawfull vnto* ἃ. Catholicke
*Conſcience ; for-ſo much, as it conteyneth ſundry clauſes
repugnant to his Religion.*

S. Hieron. Comment. in Cap. 4. Hierem.

Let an *Oath* haue theſe companions, Truth, Iudgment, and Iuſtice; for
if theſe be wanting, it ſhall not be an *Oath*, but Periury.

¶ Permiſſu Superiorum. ANNO 1608.

THE GENERALL
Contentes of this enfuing Letter,
diuided into three
Paragraphes.

1. THE *first paragraph handleth matters concerning the substance of the Oath, which in the Apologie are spoken by way, as it were, of Preface, before the setting downe of the Popes Breues.*

2. THE *second, considereth the said two Breues, & impugnation therof by the Apologer; and how sufficiently, or insufficiently, the same is performed by him.*

3. THE *third, discusseth the Answere made to* Cardinall Bellarmynes *Letter; & diuers poyntes of moment therin conteyned, but weakly impugned by the* Apologer, *as the Authour of this Letter iudgeth.*

TO

To the Reader.

His Letter comming to my hands (gentle Reader) some dayes past, from my learned friend beyond the seas, and hauing imparted the same priuately vnto sundry of myne acquaintance, who desyred to read somewhat, concerning the Argument in hãd; they were very earnest with me to yield to the printing therof, for eschewing so great labour, tyme, and expences, as would be necessary for the copying it out, to so many, as desyred the view therof: which I intreate thee to take in good part, and vse it to thy benefit. And so to CHRIST IESVS I committ thee, with wish of all felicitie, both in this lyfe, and the next.

PARTICVLER
chiefe poyntes handled in this Letter.

In the firſt Paragraph.

In

In the Second Paragraph.

In the third Paragraph.

of

THE

THE
IVDGMENT
OF A CATHOLICKE
MAN, TO HIS FRIEND
in England,

Concerning the Apology, *for the new*
Oath *of* Allegiance.

Paragr. I.

I CANNOT, but yeild yow harty thankes (my louing friend) for the new *Booke* yow sent me ouer by *Guntar*, at his last passage: For albeit, I haue determyned with my selfe in this my banishment, to spend my tyme in other studyes, more profitable, then in contention about Controuersyes: yet must I needes accept kyndly of your good will, in making me partaker of your newes there. And more gladde should I haue beene, if yow had aduertised me, what your, and other mens opinion, was of the *Booke* in your parts, then

A   that

that yow requeſt me to write our mens Iudgement from hence. And yet, for ſo much, as yow require it ſo earneſtly at my handes, and that the party is to returne preſently , I ſhall ſay ſomewhat with the greateſt breuity that I can : Albeit I do not doubt, but that the partyes, that are principally intereſſed therin , will anſwere the ſame much more largely.

II. Firſt then for the Authour, for ſo much as
About the Authour of the Apologie. he ſetteth not downe his Name , it ſeemeth not ſo eaſy to gheſſe ; yet the more generall opinion in theſe partes is, that as , that odious *Diſcouery of Roman Doctryne, and practiſes* , which of late yow haue ſeene anſwered, was caſt forth againſt the Catholickes, vnder the cyfred name of T. M: with direction (as
Tho. Morton. he ſaid) from *Superiours*, the Authour being in deed but an inferiour Miniſter ; ſo dyuers thinke it to be probable , that this other *Booke* alſo , commeth from
Tho. Montague. ſome other T. M. of like condition , though in reſpect of his office, ſomewhat neerer to his Maieſty, to whome, perhaps, he might ſhew the ſame (as the other dedicated his) and therupon might preſume to ſet it forth *Authoritate Regiâ* , as in the firſt front of the *Booke* is ſet downe, ſomwhat different from other bookes , and cauſe it to be printed by *Barker* his Maties Printer, and adorned in the ſecond page with the Kings Armes, and other like deuiſes , wherin our Engliſh *Miniſters*, do grow now, to be very bold, & do hope to haue, in tyme, the hand , which *Scottiſh* Miniſters once had. But I moſt certaynly do perſwade my ſelfe, that his Matie neuer read aduiſedly all, that in this *Booke* is conteyned : For that I take him to be of ſuch iudgement and honour, as he would neuer haue let paſſe ſundry things , that heere are publiſhed, contrary to them both.

III. As for example, his Highnes great iudgement would preſently haue diſcouered, that the State
of

of the Queſtion, is twice or thrice changed in this *Apologie*, and that thing proued by allegations of Scriptures, Fathers and Councels, which the aduerſe part denyeth not, as after in due place I ſhall ſhew. And againe he would neuer haue let paſſe, ſo manifeſt an ouerſight, as is the charging of Card.ᵃˡˡ *Bellarmine* with eleuen ſeuerall places of contradiction to himſelfe in his workes, whereas, in the true nature of a contradiction or contrariety, no one of them can be proued, or mainteyned, as euery man that vnderſtandeth the Latyn tongue, and will but looke vpon *Bellarmine* himſelfe will preſently fynd.

What his Maieſties great iudgmét would haue diſcouered, if he had read the Apology.

IV. Nay ſome of them are ſo palpable, as euery man of common ſenſe, euen without Latyn, or learning, will eſpy the ſame: as namely, the very firſt, where it is ſaid, That Card.ᵃˡˡ *Bellarmine* writeth in his fifth Booke of *Iuſtification*: That, *for the vncertainty of our owne proper righteouſneſſe, and for auoyding of vayne glory, it is moſt ſure and ſafe to repoſe our whole confidence in the alone mercy and goodnes of God.* Which propoſition (ſayth the *Apologie*) is directly contrary to the whole diſcourſe and currant of all his fyue bookes *De Iuſtificatione*. But euery man out of common reaſon, will ſay, that the oppoſition betweene one place, and fiue bookes, is very generall, and vncertayne to the Reader. He ſhould haue cyted ſome one or two, or more places, out of thoſe fyue bookes, which in true ſenſe, and wordes had byn contrary to the former place, to the end that iudgement might haue byn made therof: and this in credit he ought to haue done, to conuince ſo great a man of contradiction to himſelfe.

Cap. 7.

V. Agayne, it is alleadged for a manifeſt contradiction in *Bellarmine*, for that in one place he ſaith: That, *the end of the world can not be knowne*: and in another, That *within 25. dayes after Antichriſts death, the world ſhall haue an end.* But what man is ſo ſimple, or ſilly,

that will not prefently demaund, how we fhall know
the certaynty, when Antichrift is to come? For therupon dependeth the whole controuerfy.

V I. In like manner wheras his Matie is knowne to
be a Prince of moft honorable refpects in treaty, and
vfage of others, efpecially men of honour and dignity,
it is to be thought, that he would neuer haue con-
fented, if he had but feene the *Booke*, with any atten-
tion , that thofe phrafes of contempt, not only a-
gainft the *Pope* (at leaft as a temporall Prince) but
neyther againft the *Cardinall*, calling him by the name

What his
Maiefty in
honour
woulde
haue mif-
liked.

of *M.Bellarmine*, fhould haue paffed ; For fo much , as
both the *Emperour*, and greateft Kings of Chriftendome, do name that dignity with honour. And it
feemeth no leffe diffonant, to call a Cardinall, *Maifter*,
then if a man fhould call the chiefeft dignityes of
our Crowne by that name, as *M. Chauncelour, M. Trea-
furer, M. Duke, M. Earle, M. Archbishop, M.Bancroft*, which I
affure my felfe, his Matie would in law of honour
condemne, if any externall Subiect or Prince, fhould
vfe to men of that State in our Countrey, though he
were of different Religion. Wherfore I reft moft af-
fured, that this proceeded, eyther out of the Minifters
lacke of modeftie, or charity : and that if his Matie
had had the perufall of the *Booke* , before it came
forth, he would prefently haue gyuen a dafh of his
pen ouer it, with effectuall order to remedy fuch
ouerfightes of inciuility.

V I I. Furthermore that generall affertiue note
gyuen againft *Card.*^all *Bellarmine*, that, *VVhenfoeuer he is
preffed with any difficult argument of his Aduerfary, he careth
not to contradict himfelfe, fo he may declyne therby the prefent
ftorme*, I can hardly belieue that his Matie would haue
paffed ouer with approbation. For fo much, as it is
fo generall, as I faid , and would require an induction of many particuler examples , to inferre the
same;

same; wherof no one is heere alledged, that can be
stood vnto, and proued to be a true contradiction in
deed. That other iniurious and stinging conclusion
also, that, *There is no greater difference betweene* God *and*
Belial, *light and darknes, heauen and hell, then there is be-*
tweene the doctrine of the Scriptures, and Card.^all Bellarmines
workes, concerning the dignity of temporall Princes, I can not
imagine that the equity, and grauity of his Matie
would euer allow of it, being apparantly a passionate
exaggeration, and refuted euery where by *Bellarmine*
himselfe, where he teacheth, that temporall Princes
haue their Authority from God, are Gods substitutes
and Vicars, in all temporall affayres of their States
and Kingdomes, are for such to be obeyed, not only,
out of feare to auoyd punishment, but of conscience
vnder paynes of damnation: so as, wherin this great
and absolute opposition of *Scriptures* to *Bellarmins* works,
about the Authority and dignity of temporall Princes
doth consist, I see not. And if his bookes had byn so
derogatory to Princely Authority, as heere is said, it
is very like, that so many other Monarches, Princes,
and great States, would neuer haue permitted them to
haue bene printed in their Dominions, as they haue
done, and do dayly. Wherfore, neyther this also, do
I suppose, that the great wisedome of his Matie would
haue allowed.

Vide lib. de
Laicis, ma-
xime ca. 10.
11. &c.

VIII. This then remayneth most firme in my
persuasion, that his Matie had nothing to do with
the *Booke*, but only, perhaps, the allowance therof in
generall termes, before it was published: and this
yow will easely see by the substance therof, which
consisteth (such as it is) of three principall poynts or
partes. The first, conteynng, as it were, a preamble to
the *Breues,* concerning the nature of the *Oath* exacted,
and circumstances therof. The second, touching the
contents of the said *Breues,* & the *Popes* manner of pro-

Three par-
tes of the
Apology.

A 2   ceeding

ceeding therin. The third, the examination of Card.^{all}
Bellarmines letter to *M. Blackwell* the Arch-prieſt: of all
which, I do promiſe yow, but a ſmall taſt, as I ſaid; for
I haue very little tyme, and I ſhould offer iniury to
others, to whome it belongeth to make a more full
anſwere, if I ſhould deteyne my ſelfe long therin.

IX. The preamble beginneth with, *The monſtrous,
rare, nay neuer-heard-of treacherous, famous, and infamous attempt, plotted within theſe few yeares heere in* England *(of
the powder-treaſon) infinite in cruelty, ſingular from all example,
crying loudly for vengeance from heauen,* &c. All which Epi-
thetes for due deteſtation of ſo raſh and heynous an
attempt, Catholicks, no leſſe then Proteſtants, do willingly admit; though for ſingularity from all examples, if we reſpect *Speciem,* & non *Indiuiduum,*that cannot
be like to an other in all poynts, there be recounted
in Hiſtoryes, many attempts of the ſame kynd, and
ſome alſo by *Proteſtants,* in our dayes: as that of them,
who in *Antwerp* placed a whole barke of powder in
the vaulted great ſtreet of that Citty, where the Prince
of *Parma,* with his nobility, was to paſſe: and that of
him in *Hage,* that would haue blowne vp the whole
Counſell of *Holland,* vpon priuate reuenge: as alſo that
of *Edenburrow* in *Scotland,* where the like trayne of
powder was layd for the cruell murther of his Maties
Father, which not ſucceeding, his death was achieued
by an other, no leſſe bloudy, and barbarous, violence.

X. But why (I pray yow) is this wofull attempt
of thoſe vnfortunate Gentlemen, ſo often brought in
agayne, and repeated almoſt in euery corner of this
Booke ? Are they not executed, that were culpable
therof? And are not other Catholicks deliuered from
the guylt therof, by the long, and diligent ſearch of
Iuſtice made thereabout? The Miniſter himſelfe con-
feſſeth in his very next lynes, *The equity of his Ma.*^{tie} *to
be ſuch*

Pag.1.& 2.

The o-
dious and
oftenrepe-
tition of
the pow-
der-trea-
ſon.

be such, as he professed in his Proclamation, & Parlament-speach, that he would not vse other Catholicks the worse for that, wherof it followeth that he held them for guytlesse ; & that all those pressures both of cosciences & externall afflictiō which since that tyme they haue suffered, and do at this present, were designed before that, and begunne also to be put in execution (as indeed they were) and that the powder - treason was not a cause of these afflictions, but an effect rather : that is to say, that those Gentlemen forseeing or knowing the course that was designed to be taken, and partly also put in practice, resolued vpon that miserable *Medium* , to their owne destruction, and publike calamity.

XI. But alas, is there no end of exprobration against the Innocent for the Nocent? No compassion? No commiseration ? If the clemency of his Matie in his gratious Proclamation (as heere is confessed) gaue security, that, notwithstanding that headlong action of those few Catholycke Gentlemen, *None of the profession should be the worse vsed for that cause* ; how commeth it to passe, that so many aggrieuances haue byn heaped vpon them euer since , and are daylie, both by infamous libels published against them, as appeareth by the former T. M. his slauderous *Discouery*, and others mentioned in the Answere therunto ; as also by the new *Oath*, deuised for the vtter ouerthrow, both in soule, if they take it against their conscience, and of body, goods, and estimation, if they refuse it ? How come so many searches of their houses, spoyle of their goodes, apprehensions of their persons, afflictions of their tennants, seruants & friends, so many citations, attachments, vexations, and molestations, that dayly do flow vpon them, as if they were the only malefactours of the Land?

XII. And now I pray yow let vs see, how this second T. M. (if he be Authour of the *Booke*, as he is presumed)

The powder-treason not so much a cause, as an effect of Catholiks tribulatio.

In the treatise of Mitigation in the preface

presumed) doth speake of this *Oath*, as of a thing of no pressure & preiudice at all. For hauing spoken of

Apologia pag.2.lin. vlt.

the former asseueration of his Ma.tie, *That none of that profession should be worse vsed for that cause,* he adioyneth presently: *Only* (saith he) *at the next sitting downe againe of Parliament a forme of Oath was framed to be taken by all his Ma.*ties *Subiects, wherby they should make cleere profession of their Resolution, faithfully to persist in his Ma.*ties *Obedience, according to their naturall allegiance: To the end, that heerby his*

Pag.3.

*Ma.*tie *might make a separation of his Subiects &c.* by which exception of (*Only*) a man may well perceaue, that this Minister maketh litle accompt of taking, or not taking

The agrie-uance of this Oath.

this *Oath*, for so much as he supposeth Catholike people to haue receaued no hard vsage therby, though they be brought into such extremityes, as either they must sweare against their owne iudgements, & conscience in diuers pointes, appertayning to their Religion, or indure his Ma.ties heauy displeasure, with losse of all, that in this lyfe is dearest vnto them: which no Catholicke man can auoyd now in *England*, but he that maketh no scruple to sweare or vnsweare whatsoeuer turneth him best to his commodity, or Superior Authority doth impose vpon him.

   XIII. But against this, you will say, that two thinges heere are alledged, and auouched in his Maiesties behalfe, by the Authour of this Pamphlet: the one, that, *He intendeth no persecution against Catholickes for*

Pag. 4.

conscience cause, but only desireth to be secured of them for Ciuill Obedience: Which if it be so, I see not, but that the matter may quickly be ended: for that I presume no Catholicke in *England*, will deny to sweare all cyuill obedience that he oweth to his Maiesty, or that any subiect hath euer in former Catholicke times sworne to their leige Lords or Princes, or do in other countryes at this day. The other is, *That very many* (sayth he) *of his Maiesties subiects that were Popishly affected, as well Priests as Laycks haue*

haue freely taken the same Oath, wherby they both gaue his Maiestie *occasion to thinke the better of their fidelity & likewise freed them* *selues of that heauy slaunder.* So he. And then followeth immediatly that his Maiesty punisheth none for Conscience cause, so they exhibite Cyuill Obedience. And why then are men kept in prison, after they haue taken this Oath? Why are M. *Blackwell,* and M. *Charnocke* deteyned styll by the L. of Canterbury? Why are Recusants punished, & fyned for Recusancy, though they take the *Oath* of *Allegiance*? Is not Recusancie a cause of Conscience? Do you see how these things do hold togeather.

XIIII. To returne then to this Booke, the writer saith, *That the Dyuell could not haue deuised a more* *malitious tricke, for interrupting this so calme and clement a* *course, then by sending hither and publishing a* Breue *of the Pope,* *counter-maunding all them of his profession, to take this Oath,* *therby sowing new seedes of iealousy betweene his Maiesty and his* *Popish Subiects. &c.* But what was the calme & clement course before, all men know. For first men were vexed, spoyled, & imprisoned for Recusancy; then was the *Oath* deuised to afflict their Consciences: and in these afflictions what should Catholicks do? They first consulted the case which Learned men at home; then also abroad: And albeit at home, some were moued in respect of the compassion they had of the present perill, if it were refused, to thinke that in some sense the *Oath* might be taken: yet none abroad were of that mynd: For that they allowed not of any sort of *Equiuocation* in matters touching faith & religion. And in these, I heare say that the Iesuites were among the chiefe & most forward, as heere also is confessed: who notwithstanding before were most accused, bayted and exagitated, both in Bookes, Pulpitts, and Tribunalls, for allowing, in some points, the lawfull vse of *Equiuocation*.

The Oath consulted, both at home and abroad.

B XV.

XV. About this doubt, Catholickes, according to their rule of Subordination, and spirituall Obedience in such affayres, referring the matter to the iudgment and consultation of their Supreme *Paſtour*, whome by the principles of their Religion they beleue, that our Sauiour giueth aſſiſtance, for the direction of mens ſoules; they receyued from him, after due deliberation, this anſwere, *That the whole Oath, as it lay, could not be admitted with the integritie of the Catholicke Faith.* For that albeit diuers partes therof were lawfull, to wit, all ſuch clauſes, as appertained to the promiſe of Ciuill and Temporall Obedience: yet other thinges, being interlaced and mixt therwith, which do detract from the ſpirituall Authoritie of their ſaid higheſt Paſtour (at leaſtwiſe indirectly) the whole Oath, as it lieth, was made therby vnlawfull.

See the Breue 10. Kal. Octo. 1606.

XVI. And this I vnderſtand to be the ſubſtance of the *Popes* Reſolution and anſwere, though all theſe particularityes be not ſet downe in his *Breues*, but onely the Oath declared to be vnlawfull in conſcience to Catholicke men, as it lyeth, without diſtinction. And what *malitious tricke of the Diuell then*, this may be thought, where ſheepe do make recourſe to their ſpirituall Paſtour, in ſo great and important occaſions of their ſoules, as theſe are, I ſee not. Do Engliſh Catholickes any other thing in this, then that which all Engliſh Subiects, both great and ſmall, learned and vnlearned haue done, and practiſed from our firſt Chriſtian Kinges, vntill the time of King *Henry* the eight, vpon the point of a thouſand yeares? Let the Anſwere to Sir *Edward Cookes* booke of *Reportes* lately ſet forth, be examined, whether it doth not ſhew, that in all thoſe Ages, recourſe was euer made to the Sea *Apoſtolicke*, in like occaſions, without preiudice of Subiectes temporall dueties to their temporall Princes.

See Anſwer cap. 6.

XVII. No one Engliſh Chriſtian King (though
they

they were many) did euer abfolutly deny recourfe to *Rome* in fpirituall things (notwithftanding in fome other Cyuill, or mixt matters, vpon different occafions, fome reftraintes were fome tymes made) from our firft king *Ethelbert* to king *Henry* the eyght, as by the faid difcourfe & Anfwere is euidently proued : & much more throughout the noble rancke of the Chriftian kinges of *Scotland*, his Maties Progenitours, vntill his moft renowned Progenitrix (by whome, and from whom he hath his royall right of both Crownes) who is knowne & reputed throughout Chriftendome, to haue died for defence of this Catholicke doctrine: For fo much, as if fhe would haue abandoned that, there had byn little doubt of making her away. And the like may be faid of all other great Chriftian and Catholicke Princes of our dayes, as the Emperour himfelfe, the Potent Kings, and Monarches of *Spayne*, *France*, *Polonia*, and other States, Common-wealthes, and Potentates, do not thinke it any difgrace, diminution of honour, perill or iniury vnto them, that their Subiects, for matters of Confcience, do make recourfe to the Sea *Apoftolicke*, or that, which is confequent therof, the faid Sea, or generall Paftour do interpofe his iudgement, declaration, or decifion in fuch affayres.

XVIII. This is the Catholicke doctrine and practife : this hath bene in vfe throughout Chriftendome from all antiquity, & no where more then in our Realmes of *England* and *Scotland*, as hath byn faid. In this beliefe and practice, liued and dyed all our forfathers, that were Subiects, all our noble Kings, that were our Soueraignes, all our Bifhops and Prelats, that were our Paftours, all our great Counfellours and Lawyers, that by their wifdome and learning gouerned the land, all our Nobility, Gentry, Priefts and Laytie : So as if now this be holden for *a malitious tricke*

B 2   *of*

Recourfe to *Rome* euer vfual from our firft Chriftianity.

Q. Mary of Scotland.

Catholiks do hould & practice what all their Anceftours haue done.

of the diuell, dishonorable and preiudiciall to his Matie, his Soueraignty, Crowne, dignity and security, as heere is insinuated, it must needs be, ior that the diuell indeed hath made some change in other men, and matters, by altering of opinions and apprehensions. For the Catholicks are the same that they were wont to be, and do thinke the same, belieue the same, teach the same, and practice the same, that all their predecessors haue done before them.

XIX. But to returne to the Apologie. Two mislikes are consequently set downe, after the former wordes: *The firſt, that the* Pope *did* mittere falcem in alienam messem, *by intermedling betweene his* Matie *and his Subiects, especially in matters that meerely and only concerne cyuill Obedience.* The other, *that he refuted not particulerly, what speciall wordes he quarrelled in that Oath; which if he had done* (saith the Apologie) *it might haue byn, that his* Matie *for the Fatherly care he hath, not to put any of his Subiects to a needles extremity, might haue byn contented, in some sort, to haue reformed, or interpreted those words with his owne Catholicks, and so had they byn therby fully eafed in that busines; or at leaſtwise, some appearance or shaddow of excuse, might haue byn left vnto them for refusing the same, vpon scrupulous tendernesse of Conscience,* &c. Thus writeth he. Which if he do *bona fide,* and haue besydes any inckling or insight in his Maties meaning indeed that way, for the eafe or comfort of his afflicted Catholicke people; I doubt not, but that full satisfaction may be gyuen to his Royall Highnes, in these two poyntes that heere are set downe.

XX. For firſt, about *putting the Popes hooke in another mans harueſt,* suppofing, as we do, that wee treate of Catholicke people only, and according to Catholicke doctryne, and in matters belonging to Catholicke mens soules and confciences; it cannot be called Meſsis aliena, an other mans harueſt, that the Pope dealeth in England, with fuch kynd of people, and in fuch caufes, as well

as

Apol. pa. 6.

Ibid. pag. 7.

English Catholiks not *Meſsis aliena* to the Sea Apoſtolike.

as in *Spayne*, *France*, *Flanders*, *Italie*, *Germanie*, *Polonia*, and other States and Kingdomes; for that they are no lesse appertayning to his flocke, care, charge, and haruest, then the rest. Neyther doth the materiall separation of our Iland, separate vs from the vnion of one body, nor of one Obedience to one & the selfe same general Head and Pastour, no more, then it doth from the vnion of one beliefe, and of one number and forme of Sacraments, of one manner of seruice, and other like poyntes, belonging to the internall and externall vnitie of Catholicke Religion.

XXI. But the Apologie saith, that, *His medling about this Oath, is in matters, that meerly and only concerne Cyuill Obedience*: and the same he repeateth in dyuers other partes and passages of this *Booke*; which if it be true, I will easely graunt that his Matie hath cause of iust mislike. But if this proue not so, and that the matters refused in the *Oath*, are poyntes appertayning in deed to Religion, then I hope, that by answering fully this poynt, we shall satisfy also the second, why it was not needfull for the Pope to set downe any particuler confutation in his *Breues*, but only to say (as he doth) in generall, that, *The integrity of Catholicke Religion permitteth them not to take such an Oath*, in which, both Cyuill and Ecclesiasticall poynts are couched, and conioyned craftily togeather, with no small preiudice of the said Catholicke Religion.

Ibid. pag.6.

XXII. And how the shall we cleare this importāt matter, *VVhether there be any pointes in this Oath belonging to religion, besydes Cyuill Obedience?* Very easily : by foure seuerall, and distinct wayes. The first wherof shall be taken from the playne expresse wordes, sense, and drift of the Oath it selfe: That besydes the acknowledgment of our Soueraigne *to be true King, and rightfull Lord ouer all his dominions*, and that, *I will be a true loyall Subiect vnto him*, and other such like clauses, wherat no man sticketh or maketh difficulty; the said *Oath* conteyneth further, that,

B 3. I must

That the
Oath con-
teyneth
poyntes
againſt Ca-
tholicke
Religion.

I *muſt ſweare in like manner ſome poyntes concerning the limitation of the Popes authority*, to wit, *what he cannot do towards his* Matie *or his Succeſſours in any caſe whatſoeuer.* Which queſtion being brought from the particuler *Hypotheſis*, to the generali *Theſis*, concerning all Kings (for the like reaſon is alſo in others) both in the one & the other; it toucheth a poynt of doctryne and Catholicke beliefe, concerning the ſufficiency of Paſtorall authority, left by our Sauiour in his Church vnto S. *Peter* and his ſucceſſours, for redreſſing of all inconueniéces that may fall out, which I (being a Catholicke) *cannot in my Conſcience forſweare, without perill of euerlaſting damnation.* And this is one way of cleering the queſtion.

XXIII. An other is, to looke vpon the Popes wordes in his *Breues*, wherby will appeare, what his meaning was of the contents of the *Oath.* Wee haue heard (*ſaith he*) how yow are compelled by moſt grieuous puniſhments ſet before yow, to go to the Churches of Hereticks, to frequent their Aſſemblyes, to be preſent at their Sermons, &c. Wherby we are moued by the Zeale of our Paſtorall Office, and by the Paternail ſollicitude which we haue for the ſaluatió of your ſoules, to warne, & pray yow, in no ſorte, to go to the ſaid Churches, nor to heare their Sermons, nor to comunicate with them in any externall rytes, leaſt yow do incurre the wrath of God therby. For that, *it is not lawfull for yow to do theſe things without detriment of Gods ſeruice, and of your owne ſaluation:* as alſo yow may not, without moſt euident, and grieuous iniury of Gods honour, *bynd your ſelfe with the Oath*, which in like manner to our great griefe, we haue heard, to be adminiſtred vnto yow, of the tenour vnder written, &c. And then after the whole forme of the *Oath* ſet downe, he writeth thus. *VVhich things being ſo, it ought to be cleere vnto yow, by the wordes themſelues, that ſuch an Oath can not be taken without domage to the Catholicke fayth, and health of your ſoules: for that*

The Popes
wordes in
his Breue.

it

i conteyneth many things against the said Catholike faith, and health of your soules.

XXIV. By these wordes of the *Breue*, we may see plainly, that as the matter of going to Church, Assemblyes, and Sermons of those of a contrary Religion, are forbidden by him, as spirituall matters, and acts of a false Religion: so is the taking of the *Oath*, not in regard of Temporall & Cyuill Obedience to his Ma.tie (which by a former *Breue* his predecessour had permitted, and recommended to all Catholicks soone after his Highnes entrance vnto the Crowne; but for the admixture of other clauses, appertayning to some poyntes of Religion as before hath byn said.

XXV. The third proofe may be taken out of the ensuing letter of *Card.*all *Bellarmine*, who hauing diligently considered with other learned men, of the nature of this *Oath*, doth therfore hold it to be vnlawfull, for that it is so compounded by artificiall ioyning togeather of Temporall and Spirituall things, Cyuill Obedience, and forswearing the *Popes* authority, as (to vse his wordes) *No man can professe his Cyuill Subiection, and detest treason and conspiracy (by this Oath:) but he must be forced also to renounce the Primacy of the Sea Apostolicke.* And therfore he compareth it to the crafty composition, and commixture of Images of the Emperour *Iulian*, & of the Paynim Gods, so coupled and combined togeather in his Imperiall banner, as dutifull Subiects that were Christiās, & desyred to performe their Temporall duety & Cyuill honour to their Soueraigne, could not bow downe to his Picture, as the fashion was, but must seeme also to do the same to the heathen Idols: which rather then they would do, they were content to suffer cruell death. So as in this case such as denyed to obey in that point, did it not for lacke of reuerence, and loyall affection to their Emperour, as odiously it was obiected and amplified against them: but by reason of the mixture of

things

Cardinall Bellarmines iudgement of the contents of the Oath.

things vnlawfull, with thofe that were lawfull: And the like plainly is heere in this cafe, where Catholicks are wrongfully accufed to deny their acknowledgment of cyuill Obedience conteyned in this *Oath*, for that they refufe to take the fame : wheras their refufall is not for this, but for other claufes pertayning to their Religion.

XXVI. Fourthly then, for a more full, and fynall cleering of this matter, I can thinke of no better, nor more forcible meane, then to make this reall offer, on the behalfe of euery Englifh Catholicke, for better fatisfaction of his Matie in this poynt, fo much vrged of their Cyuill & Temporall Obedience. Firft that he will fweare, and acknowledge moft willingly, all thofe partes, and claufes of the *Oath*, that do any way appertaine to the Ciuill, and Temporall Obedience due to his Matie, whome he acknowledgeth for his true and lawfull kyng and Soueraigne ouer all his Dominions, and that he will fweare vnto him, as much loyalty, as euer any Catholicke Subiect of England, did vnto their lawfull King in former tymes, and ages, before the change of king *Henry* the eyght: or that any forraine Subiect oweth, or ought to fweare to any Catholicke *Prince* whatfoeuer at this day.

XXVII. Secondly that for the *Pope*, who, by the force of Catholicke Religion, is the Supreme *Paftour* of his foule, he hopeth in Gods goodnes, that he will neuer attempt any thing in preiudice of his Matie, nor will he euer procure, of his part, that he do: but rather will feeke to ftay, or let the fame, as much as fhall lye in his power ; praying hartily for them both. But for fo much, as the Queftion of his Authority, what he might do, in certayne vrgent cafes, for the preferuation of any Countrey; and for the vniuerfall good of Gods Church, is a matter belonging to doctrine & Religion, he cannot with fafety of his Confcience

A loyall offer of ciuill Obedience, made by Catholiks to his Maiefty.

science sweare vnto the Articles and branches of the *Oath* touching that poynt.

XXVIII. Heere then wee see that all Ciuill Obedience, and humble acknowledgment of all Temporall Duety is offered to his Maiestie by his Catholicke Subiects, in most ample manner, that can be deuised, or that is offered to any Christian Catholicke Prince lyuing. And if this be not accepted, then is it euident, that more is required, *then meere and only Ciuill Obedience*, as heere is often auouched.

Apol. pag. 4.

XXIX. And now, for so much as it is said heere in like manner, *That very many of his Ma.*ties *Subiects, that were Popishly affected, as well Priests as Laycks, did freely take the same Oath*(which he calleth *A blessed successe frō God of this godly and wyse intent, in deuising and proposing the same :*) I shall be forced also to say somwhat of this matter, before I passe any further. And first of all, concerning the freedome, wherby it is heere said, *That priests and Laycks did freely take the same*; no man, I thinke, will deny, but that the taking of this *Oath* is proposed by the Statute it selfe vnder paine of the losse of all goods and lands, and perpetuall imprisonment to him, that shall refuse it: which is the very same freedome, and no other that a merchant hath in a tēpest, eyther to cast out his goodes into the sea, for lightening his ship, or to be drowned himselfe. And though *Aristotle* in his *Ethicks* do seeme to hold it to be *Simpliciter inuoluntarium*, simply againsst the will of the doer, and Catholicke Deuynes, That it is *Inuoluntarium secundum quid*, in part inuoluntary and simply voluntary, for that, all circumstances considered, he resolueth fynally to be the best to cast out his goods and saue himselfe: yet all agree in this, that freedome is taken away by this constraint of the passion of feare: For that freedome requyreth full liberty to both extreames or obiects, that are proposed; which is not

Whether the taking of this Oath by Catholicks be a blessing from God.

1.
Statut. 3. Iacobi Reg. cap. 4.

2.*Ethic. c. 2.*

D. Thom. 1. 2. q. 6. art. 6. & Valētia, Vasquez, &c. in eum locum.

C   in

in our cafe. For that the difpleafure of the Prince, the loffe of goods and liberty, the ruyne of his family, the terrour and perfwafion of his friendes, are heauie poyfes, and do mightily preponderate on the one fide: and confequently the mention of this freedome, might haue beene pretermitted, for fo much, as no conftraint of humane will can be greater, then this: And yet is it faid in the *Oath*, that he muft do it, *both willingly and hartily, and as he belieueth in Confcience*. Let the difcreete Reader confider what coherence there is in their tale.

XXX. Secondly, as for that multitude of Priefts, & Laycks, which he fayeth, *Haue freely taken this Oath*; as their freedome was that, which now I haue mentioned, and a principall motiue (as may be prefumed) the defyre they had, to giue his Matie fatisfaction, and deliuer themfelues, and others fo much as lay in them, from that inference of difloyall meaning, which vpon the denyall therof, fome do vfe to make: fo I cannot, but in charity affure my felf, that they being Catholicks tooke the faid *Oath* (for fo much as concerneth the Popes authority in dealing with temporall Princes) in fome fuch lawfull fenfe, and interpretation, as (being by them expreffed, and accepted by the Magiftrate) may ftand with the integrity, and fincerity of true Catholicke doctrine, and faith: To witt, that the *Pope* hath not Authority without iuft caufe, to proceed againft them: *Quia illud poffumus, quod iure poffumus*, faith the law: Our authority is limited by Iuftice. Directly alfo the Pope may be denyed to haue fuch authority againft Princes, but indirectly only, *in ordine ad fpiritualia*, and when certayne great, importat, & vrgent cafes, concerning Chriftian religion fall out, which we hope will neuer be, betweene our Soueraigne, and the Sea Apoftolicke; for fo much as they haue paft already, many yeares (though in different Religions) in

peace

(margin notes)

How freely the Oath is taken.

2.

The fenfe & meaning of Catholicks, that tooke the Oath.

peace , and quietnes euen since his Matie began first
to raigne.

XXXI. But concerning the generall Question , to
deny simply and absolutely , *That the Pope is supreme Pa-*
stour of the Catholicke Church , hath any authoritie left him by
Christ , eyther directly or indirectly, with cause,or without cause, in
neuer so great a necessity, or for neuer so great and publicke an vti-
lity of the Christian Religion, to proceed against any Prince what-
soeuer temporally , for his restraint or amendment , or to permitt
other Princes to doe the same : this, I suppose, was neuer their
meaning that tooke the *Oath,*for that they should therby contradict the generall consent of all Catholicke
Deuines , and confesse , that Gods prouidence , for
the conseruation , and preseruation of his Church ,
and Kingdome vpon earth , had bene defectuous, for that he should haue left no lawful remedy ,
for so great and excessiue an euill, as that way might
fall out.

XXXII. Wherefore, for so much as some such moderate meaning, must nedes be presumed, to haue bene
in those that tooke the *Oath,*for safeguard of their Consciences ; if it might please his Maiesty to like well, and
allow of this moderation , and fauourable interpretation , as all forreyne Catholicke Kings and Monarchs
doe,without any preiudice at all of their safety,dignity,
or Imperiall preheminence : I doubt not but he should
fynd most ready conformity in all his said English Catholicke Subiects, to take the said *Oath* , who now haue
great scruple & repugnance of Conscience therin: both
for that the chiefest learned men of their Church, doe
hold the same for vtterly vnlawfull, being mixed and
compounded,as it is, and the voyce of their chiefe Pastour, to whome by the rules of their Religion, they
thinke themselues bound to harken in like cases, hath
vtterly condemned the same: and the very tenour of the
Oath it self, and last lines therof are , *That euery one shall*

An hüble
petition to
his Maiesty
for exposi-
tion of the
Oath.

C 2   *sweare*

sweare without any Equiuocation, or mentall reseruation at all, that
is to say, hartily, willingly, & truely vpon the true faith
of a Chriſtian. Which being ſo, they ſee not how they
may take the ſaid *Oath* in truth of Cōſciēce: for ſo much,
as they find no ſuch willingnes in their harts, nor can
they induce themſelues in a matter ſo neerly concerning
the Confeſſion of their faith, to Equiuocate or ſweare in
any other ſenſe, then from his Maieſty is propoſed:
and therefore doe thinke it leſſe hurt to deny plainly,
and ſincerely to ſweare, then by ſwearing, neither to
giue ſatisfaction to God, nor to his Maieſty, nor to
themſelues, nor to their neighbours. And ſo much of
this point.

3.

XXXIII. There followeth an other, which is the
third, about this matter, where this Apology ſaieth,
That God did bleſſe this godly deuiſe and intent (of making and
vrging this *Oath*) *by the admittance thereof by ſo many Prieſts &
Laicks: &c.* Which bleſſing (if it be a bleſſing) muſt concerne eyther the takers, or the exhibitours, or both. But
for the takers, what inward bleſſing of comfort in conſcience they may haue receaued thereby, I know not:
But for outward bleſſing, I ſee ſmall, for they remaine,
either in priſons, or vnder preſſures ſtill, as hath bene
ſaid. But for others of the ſame Religion that cannot
frame their Conſciences to take the ſaid *Oath,* and yet
would gladly giue his Royall Maieſty contentment &
ſatisfaction, ſo farre as they might, without offending
God; I can aſſure yow, that it is the greateſt affliction
of mynd, among other preſſures, that euer fell vnto
them. For that no violence, is like to that, which is
laied vpon mens Conſciences; for ſo much, as it lyeth in
a mās owne will & reſolutiō, to beare all other oppreſſions whatſoeuer, whether it be loſſe of goods, honours,
dignityes, yea of life it ſelf: but the oppreſſion of the
Conſcience, no man may beare patiently, though he
would neuer ſo faine. For if he yield therein, he offen-
deth

The vr-
ging of the
Oath, how
heauy a
preſſure to
Catholicks
of tender
conſciēces.

deth God , and leeseth his soule : neyther doth *Metus cadens in conſtantem virum* , feare that may terrify euen a conſtant man, excuſe in this behalfe, as appeareth by the example of the auncient Martyrs , who were forced , vnder paine of damnation, to ſtand out to death againſt all humaine power , vexations , torments, and higheſt violence, rather then to doe, ſay, or ſweare any thing againſt their Conſcience . To all theſe men then , which are thowſands in our Countrey , that neuer thought otherwiſe then to be good Subiects to his Maieſty, the deuiſing of this new *Oath* , was no bleſſing, but an vnſpeakeable affliction , and angariation of mynd.

XXXIV. To the exhibitours alſo , I ſee not what bleſſing it could be, or can be, ſo extremely to vex other men without any profit , or emolument to themſelues, or to his Maieſtyes ſeruice , which herin they would pretend to aduaunce. For if there be any cauſe of doubt, of loyall good will in them , that are forced to ſweare againſt their conſciences : much more cauſe and reaſon may there be of like doubt, after they haue ſo ſworne, then before. For that the griefe of their new wound of conſcience remayning ſtill within them, and ſtirring them to more auerſion of hart, for the iniury receaued, muſt needes worke contrary effects to that which is pretended. And whoſoeuer will not ſticke to ſweare againſt his conſcience for feare, fauour, or ſome other like paſſion, may be preſumed , that he will as eaſily breake his *Oath*, after he hath ſworne, vpon like motiues, if occaſions doe mooue him. And among all other paſſions, none is more ſtrong, then that of reuenge for oppreſſions receaued : So as we read of the whole Monarchy of *Spaine* ouerthrowne , and giuen to the *Mores*, for one paſſion of Count *Iulian*, wherby he deſired to be reuenged of his King *Roderiquez*. Nothing then is gotten in this behalfe of

Nothing gayned at all by enforcing the Oath, but much loſt.

Roder. Toletan. lib. 3. hiſt. Hiſp. cap. 18.

loyall

loyall good will, by fuch extreame preſſures, but much
rather loſt.

XXXV. But befides all this, is the grieuous ſinne
which they commit, who force, & preſſe other men to
ſweare againſt their conſciences, then which, almoſt
nothing can be imagined more heinous: for it is to
thruſt men headlong (eſpecially ſuch as are fearfull)
into the very precipitation and downfall of hell it ſelfe.
For it is the higheſt degree of ſcandall actiue, ſo much
1. Cor. 8.
Rom. 14.
Matth. 18. condemned and deteſted in Scriptures, and ſo dredfully
threatned by our Sauiour, to be feuerely puniſhed in the
life to come: for that ſcandalizing properly, is nothing
elſe, but laying a ſtumbling-block for other men to fall,
and breake their necks. And ſuch a one is this formall
Oath, which conteyneth diuers things lawfull for a Catholicke to ſweare and other things vnlawfull: and he
is forced by terrour to paſſe ouer, and ſwallow downe
the one with the other, without diſtinction, with
mani eſt repugnance of his Conſcience; which repugnance to him, is alwaies a ſynne, & damnable in ſuch
a publicke and weighty action, though the matter
were lawfull in it ſelf, and conſequently alſo vnto them,
that force him to the ſame, eyther knowing or ſuſpe-
How grie-
uous a
ſynne it is
to force
men to
ſweare a
gainſt their
conſc.éces. cting his ſaid repugnance of Conſcience. For he that
ſhould force a Iew, or Turke to ſweare, that there were
a bleſſed Trinity, eyther knowing or ſuſpecting that
they would doe it againſt their Conſcience, ſhould
ſynne grieuouſly, by forcing them to committ
that ſynne. This is Catholicke doctrine, which I
alſo thinke the learned Proteſtants themſelues will not
deny.

XXXVI. Here if any man obiect, that among vs
alſo men are vrged to take Oathes, and to abiure their
opinions in the tribunalls of Inquiſitions, and the like;
and conſequently in this *Oath* they may be forced vnder
puniſhment to abiure the Popes Temporall Authority

in dealing with Kings : I answere first , that if any Hereticke, or other should be forced to abiure his opinions , with repugnance of conscience , it should be a synne to the inforcers , if they knew it, or suspected it . Neyther is it practised or permitted in any Catholicke Court , that euer I knew. But yow will reply , that if he doe it not , he shall be punished by death , or otherwise, as the crime requireth , and Canons appoint , and consequently the like may be vsed towards Catholickes , that will not renounce their old opinions of the Popes Authoritye : but heere is a great difference ; for that the Catholicke Church hath *Ius acquisitum* , auncient right ouer Hereticks, as her due Subiects, for that by their Baptisme , they were made her Subiects , and left her afterward , and went out of her; and she vseth but her auncient manner of proceeding against them , as against all other of their kynd and quality from the beginning . But the Protestant Church of *England* hath *Nullum Ius acquisitum* vpon Catholicks , that were in possession before them , for many hundred yeares, as is euident. Neyther was there euer any such Oath exacted at their hands , by any of their Kings , in former Catholicke tymes : Neyther is there, by any Catholicke forreyne Monarch, now liuing vpon earth, and consequently , by no reason or right at all, can English Catholicke men , be eyther forced or pressed to this Oath against their Conscience , or be punished, beaten, or destroyed , if for their Conscience they refuse to take the same : humbly offering notwithstanding to their Soueraigne, to giue him all other dutifull satisfaction , for their Temporall Obedience and Allegiance , which of loyall Catholicke Subiectes may be exacted . And this shall suffice for this first point , concerning the contents

Obiections answered.

tents and nature of the *Oath*. Now shall
we passe to say somewhat of the
Breues, and answere made
thereunto.

CON-

CONCERNING
THE
POPES TVVO BREVES,
A G A I N S T
The receauing of the *Oath*.

Paragr. I I.

HE fumme of the Popes two *Breues* the firft of the 21. of September, Anno 1606. the fecond of the 21. of Auguft the next yeare following, is this: That wheras he had heard, that the Catholicks of *England*, were very forely preffed with a new de-uifed *Oath*, againft their Confcieces, concerning certayne poyntes, appertayning to the Au-thority of the Sea Apoftolicke, in fome cafes; he wrote the firft *Breue*, to admonifh, comfort, and direct them; fignifying his harty forie for their long continued affli-ctions, and exhorting them to patience, and conftancy in defence of the integrity of Catholike faith, and the

The fumme of the two Bre-ues.

D   purity

purity of their owne confciences. And a'ter this fetting
downe *verbatim* the whole *Oath*, as it lyeth in the Statute,
he condemneth the taking therof, as vnlawfull vnto a
Catholicke man, in regard of diuers claufes therin conteyned, contrary to the faid integrity of Catholicke
faith, and health of foules; though in particuler, he
defcendeth not to difpute, or difcuffe the reafons, or
poyntstherof, as became not a Iudge : efpecially feeing
(as he faith) the matters themfelues be euident by the
wordes of the *Breue*. And wheras this firlt *Breue* was
foone after called into queftion by fome, as not proceeding from the Popes owne motion, and intention :
his fecond *Breue* was fet forth to approue, ratify,
and confirme the former; affuring all Catholicks, that
both the one, and the other came from him directly,
fincerely, & vpon due deliberation, and confequently,
that they were to be acknowledged, and obeyed by all
true Catholicke people. This is the fumme of what
the Pope wrote : now lett vs fee, what aduantage is
taken by the Apologer againft the fame.

II. Firft of all he iefteth at the Popes forrow for
Catholicks afflictions, making them to be none at all :
and wheras the late *Q. Elizabeth* is not fo much as named
in eyther of thefe *Breues*, this man will needes bring her
in perforce, and iuftifie her actions againft Catholicke
people, therby the more to animate his Matie to follow
her example, fetting downe this notorious falfe po-
fition concerning her, and her doings, *That according*
to his owne knowledge, her Matie *neuer punifhed any Papift for*
Religion. Which how he can iuftify, or by what E-
quiuocation mantayne, I know not. But being not
content with this, he paffeth further, and rageth ex-
ceedingly againft thofe innocent Priefts, Students, and
others, that only for the profeffion of their Religion,
gaue vp their lyues vnder her, as by their inditements,
and arraignements in publike record doth appeare, and
conclu-

Apolog.
pag.16.

concludeth finally both of her, and them, thus: *This Gracious Princesse was as free from persecution, as these hellish Instruments from the honour of Martyrdome.* And yet further, very profanely: *Hauing now sacrificed, as I may say* (quoth he) *to the Manes of my defunct Soueraigne, as well for the discharge of my particuler duty, as loue of verity; I must next performe my duty also to his Ma.*^{tie} *present, &c.*

III. Wherunto a man might answere, that if he performe it with no more verity to his *present Soueraigne,* then he hath done to his *defunct Soueraigne past ;* he will gayne little grace (I suppose) with his Matie whom I hold to be of that noble nature, and magnanimity, as that he taketh such grosse-lying-flattery, rather for iniury, then obsequie. But as for his heathen, prophane sacrificing to the *Manes* or Hob-gob-lins of his late Lady; I confesse, that it is an office fitter for a Protestant-Minister, that thinketh it vnlawfull to pray for her soule, to deale with her *Manes* or Infernal spirits, then with Celestiall, by praying for her to Saints. But would God these *Manes* might now haue licence to appeare, and talke with him, and relate what passeth with her after all this ioylity, and ruffe in this world; I doubt not but they would coole his excessiue veyne of flattering vanity. For if all the old platforme of Saints lyues, prescribed in Scriptures and practised by seruants of God, were not erroneous & vayne, as much fasting, continuall prayer, dayly mortification, frequent recollection, diligent chasticement of their bodyes, humble and feruent deuotion, labouring and working saluation in feare and trembling, aboundant almesdeedes, haire-cloth and ashes, contrition, sorrow and sobbing for synnes: If these things (I say) were the ancient wayes to lyfe, and to euerlasting saluation: then must the pathes of *Q. Elizabeth,* which are knowne by most men, to haue byn, eyther wholy different, or most opposite to these, lead to an other opposite end, *Quia vnus-*

See Stowes Chronicle in the death of *M. Mayne* anno 1577. of *M. Nelson* anno 1578. of *M. Shirwood* anno 1578. of *M. Hanse* 1581. &c. *Apol.* Pag. 18.

Q. Elizabeth her *Manes.*

D 2

vnufquifque recipiet , fecundum opera fua.

IV. But not to enter into thefe melancholicke matters of her *Manes*, or of the other world, to make any certayne iudgement therof, before we arryue thither: I will only fpeake a word or two of the world prefent, and this with proteftation, that it is wholy againft my will, and againft the generall inclination (as I take it) of all Catholicke people, who would in charity be content, that the memory of her actions,& iniuryes againft them, being neuer fo many , & iniurious,were buried with her body; as may well appeare by their long filence therin fince her death. But the continuall egging of the aduerfary is fuch, as forceth vs to fay fomwhat, for our owne defence, and for cleering the caufe, and men, by her fo eagerly and iniurioufly purfued,

Apol. pag.
16.

V. This Minifter then, as in part you haue heard, maketh her, *The moft myld , dolce, patient, and clement Princeffe in the world* , euen vnto Catholicks , whofe bloud fhe fhed fo aboundantly, both at home, & abroad, during all the time of her raigne : nay, *That her Ma.*tie *neuer punifhed any Papift for religion:* And, That fhe was *moft free from all perfecution: That fhe neuer medled with hard punifhment of any Catholicke, nor made any rigorous lawes againft them before the excommunication of Pope Pius Quintus*, that was in the eleuenth yeare of her raigne : And yet is it knowne, and cannot be denyed, but that the moft grieuous law, & *Oath* of *Supremacie*, & rigorous penall Statute againft faying, or hearing Maffe, were made long before that tyme : And that all the Bifhops, Prelates, Religious, & chiefe Ecclefiafticall men were depryued, fpoyled, imprifoned, or forced into banifhment : and this before the Pope vfed any Cenfure againft her at all : fo exact, & punctuall is the truth of this Minifters narration. And not content with this, he doth profecute odious comparifons, betweene the Pope,& her, laying all the

See Sâders
lib.7.de Ec-
clefiaftica
Monarchia:
who fetteth down
the particuler perfons.

origen

origen of hurts and wickednes to him, and merit of vertue, and innocency to her, which is the very same, that is mentioned by the Prophet, *to call eu'll good, & good euil.*

Isa.5.

VI. Nor is he alone in this deuise, but that all Mini-sters commonly, and Ministers mates of later dayes haue taken vp this Common place, to celebrate her high praylcs, for difgrace o Catholicks. And one among the rest, that for his place, should haue more equity and discretiō, hath declaymed vpon this matter in publicke Audience more then once, especially vpon the occasion of certayn words in *Pope* Clements *Breue*, where she is named *Misera Famina*, a miserable woman (in respect no doubt of the myseries of her soule, little respected by her:) vpon which words the *Orator* triumpheth thus, *VVhat miserable? It is said, That*, Miseria constat ex duobus contrariis, copia & inopia, copia tribulationis, & ino-pia consolationis, *Misery consisteth of two contraries,. of aboundance, and penury, aboundance of tribulation, & penury of con-solation.* And then he sheweth in what aboundance of consolations Q. *Elizabeth* lyued in all her life, & with-out want of all tribulations: which if it were true; yet is it but the argument which the worldlings vsed in the Psalme, to proue their felicity, that their cellars are full, their sheepe fertile, theyr kyne fatt, they suffer no losse: and then, *Beatum dixerunt populum cui hæc sunt;* Happy did they call the people that had these things. But the Holy Ghost scorneth them, and so may all men do our Orator, that vseth and vrgeth so base an argument, in so high a matter.

Lo. Cooke in the booke of the late Arraigne-ments fol. 63.

Psalm. 143.

VII. And as for his definition of *Miserie*, by *Copia* and *Inopia*, store and want, it is a miserable one indeed, and neuer heard of before, I thinke, to come from any mans mouth, but his owne: it being ridiculous in Philosophy, and fitt to be applyed to any thing that hath either store or want: As a wise man in this sort

may be defined to be him, that hath ſtore of witt, and
want of folly ; and a foole to be him, that hath ſtore
of follie, and want of witt ; and ſo a rich man is he that
hath ſtore of riches and want of beggary ; and a poore
man is he, that hath ſtore of beggary, and penury of
riches. And are not theſe goodly definitions (thinke
you) for ſo great and graue a man to produce?

Cooke ib.
pag. 64.

VIII. But to returne to the matter it ſelfe of Q.
Elizabeth her ſtore of conſolations, and penury of deſo-
lations in this life , *VVho* (ſaith this our Orator) *was
ſo myraculouſly protected by God, ſo ſtrengthened and fortified, as
ſhe did beate her moſt potent enemy, did ſett vp a King in his kingdome, defended nations, harboured diſtreſſed people , and the like.*
Suppoſing all this were true, that ſhe had ſuch temporall felicity in this lyfe, and were ſo miraculouſly protected, ſtrengthened, and fortifyed by God as heere is
ſaid : yea and that it were euident, that God had cho-
ſen her for his elected ſeruant (which yet doth not
appeare) and gyuen her that tytle and power, to afflict
the Catholicks: yet had that byn no more, then we read
in the Scriptures to haue byn gyuen to dyuers Pagan
Princes, and namely to *Nabuchodonoſor* , of whom *Ieremy*
the prophet teſtifyeth in ſundry places of his Propheſy,
That God choſe him, called him his ſeruant, and gaue
him ſpeciall power, fauour, & protection to afflict his

Hier. 27.6.
"
"
"
"
"
"
"
Hier. 25.9.
"
"

people. *Ego dedi omnes terras iſtas in manu Nabuchodonoſor Regis
Babylonis ſerui mei,* ſaith God : I haue gyuen all theſe
Countryes into the hands of *Nabuchodonoſor* King of
Babylon my ſeruant, and all nations ſhall ſerue him , &
yield obedience to him, and to his Sonne, and Sonnes
ſonne : And what ſoeuer nation ſhall not ſerue him, &
bow his necke vnder his yoke, I will viſite that nation
with the ſword, with famyne, and with plague, till I
haue conſumed them by his hand. *And agayne in an other
place:* I will chooſe vnto me my ſeruāt *Nabuchodonoſor* king
of *Babylon,* & will bring him vpon this Land, and vpon
　　　　　　　　　　　　　　　　　　　　　　　all

all the inhabitants therof, and vpon all nations round „
about &c. And yet further God faid vnto *Ieremy:* Thus „
faith the Lord oi *Hoftes,* I fhall take vnto me my feruant „
Nabuchodonofor, and fhall place his throne vpon thefe „
ftones &c. „

IX. By all which is euident that *Syr Edward Cookes*
argument is worth nothing: that for fo much as God
fo miraculoufly protected *Q. Elizabeth,* (it it were myracu-
lous,) fo ftrengthened, and fortifyed her, as fhe did beate
her moft potent enemy, & did fet vp an other King in
his Kingdome (if any fuch thing were:) yet this did not
make her happie. As neyther it did *Nabuchodonofor,* of
whome God faid in the fame place, that when he had
ferued his turne of him, and wrought his will by his
hand, and people, for the purging of his owne elect;
he would vifit vpon him alfo, and his Countrey, and
that in a farre more grieuous fort: *Ponam illam in folitu-*
dines fempiternas, & reddam eis fecundum opera eorum, & fecun-
dum facta manuum fuarum: I fhall make that Countrey, an
euerlafting wildernes, and fhall reftore to them (that afflicted my people) according to their workes, and to the
deeds of their owne handes againft my people. This
then was his felicity to be a fcourge to others, and fynally alfo to himfelfe moft of all.

X. And the like, I doubt not, may be faid of *Q. Eliza-*
beths felicity againft Catholicks, if we knew all, that in
the laft day of iudgment will appeare, and wherof her
lamerable end may gyue great prefage to them that are
wife. For that for a woman of fo long and large a
lyfe, as hers was, to paffe hence to eternity with fo fmall
fenfe or feeling of God, as neuer fo much, as to name
him, nor to fuffer * others to bring in any fpeach therof,
as they attempted to do, is fo pittifull an end, as can
lightly fall to a Chriftian foule: The ftory of which
vpſhot of hers, I haue read written by a perfon of much
credit that was prefent at all her laft ficknes, combats,
and

How Na-
buchodo-
nofor was
the feruant
of God.

Hier. 25.11.

* Archb. of
Canterb.

and death, and relateth all that paſſed as an eye witneſſe, which I paſſe ouer for breuity and modeſtyes ſake; but it will remayne to poſterity, as a dreadfull patterne of a miſerable end, after a lyfe of ſo much ioylitie.

XI. And thus much for ſpirituall infelicityes, reaching to the next world, and lyfe or death to come. But if we would reſt our ſelues only vpon vayne & brickle felicityes of this world, they were not (alas) ſo great in Queene *Elizabeth*, but that they were mingled and interlaced with many, and great infelicityes in like manner, and theſe ſuch, as did euen in the eyes of worldly men, ouerpoiſe the other, eſpecially with them that repute honour and diſhonour among humane felicityes, & infelicityes. For what more diſhonorable infelicity can there be, then that which ſtandeth *in Capite Libri* of Q. *Elizabeths* lyfe? To witt, the publike ſolemne Statute, and Act of *Parliament*, made within few dayes after ſhe was borne, vpon the 28. yeare of King Henryes raigne, and yet extant in Print, wherin it is declared, not only by the iudgment of the King, and of all that Parliament, but by the iudiciall ſentence alſo of Archbiſhop *Cranmer*, ſhe was pronounced, *to be vnlawfully borne, and that her mother was neuer King Henryes lawfull wyfe*: wherupō the ſaid ſtatute vſeth theſe wordes: *That it was againſt all honour, equity, and good conſcience, that the ſaid Elizabeth ſhould ſucceed in the Imperiall Crowne of* England. And could there be any greater worldly infelicity thē this.

XII. I let paſſe many other infelicities, which happened by her occaſion to ſundry, as well vnder the raigne of King *Edward*, as the ruyne of the *Seymers* vpon the Admiralls falling in loue with her, and making away his former wife *Queene Catherine Parre* to enioy her; as alſo vnder Queene *Marie*, when ſo many rebellions of *VViat, Courtney, Careures, Stafford,* & others, were made for her. But her owne raigne had moſt infelicities for her, if

they

Queene Elizabeth her felicityes mingled with infelicities.

Q. Eli. her diſhonourable birth an. 28. Stat. Cap. 7.

they were well confidered: and I could touch many, but
modeftie forbiddeth. And leaft I fhould feeme to fpeak
out of reuenge, let this one confideration ferue for all;
That after all her afflicting Catholicks, and by that
exercife, vpon the egging of others, more then of her
owne propenfion, fhe was drawne into continuall fu-,
fpitions, feares, and frights of her mynd and fpirit,
euen in the midft of all thefe fenfuall delights, & con-
tentments (admired fo much by her Attorney) which
draue her to a point, wherunto by nature fhe was not
thought much inclyned, and by profeffion and proteftations, fhe moft condemned in others, to wit,
Cruelty, which in effect was fuch, out of the forefaid
feares, towards Catholicke Religion, as neuer perhaps
(yea without perhaps) were fo many feuerall lawes,
& punifhments deuifed by any one perfecutour, nor
many putt togeather, as are extant of hers in Print,
againft the profeffours of that Religion, wherof herfelfe
had byn one, and in fecret or priuate fpeaches alfo
would not deny, to be in fundry poyntes, euen to
her dying day. And was not this a great infelicity?
When ftragers do read & behold her Edicts & Statutes,
wherin not only the whole vfe of Catholicke Religion
is condemned, and vnder greiuous punifhment prohibited: but men are forced alfo, by rigorous penall lawes
to go to the Churches of a contrary Religion, to com-
municate with them, to do acts, and fweare againft
their owne Religion, faith and Confciences: that there
are feuere punifhments, of loffe of goods and lands, for
receyuing an *Agnus Dei*, or a *Medall*, or *Crucifix*: greiuous
punifhments, for keeping of a Catholicke feruant, or
Schoolemaifter to teach and bring vp their children,
or to fend them ouer feas to Catholicke Schooles: yea,
that it is the payne of death it felfe to be reconciled, by
confeffing his fynnes to the Roman Church, or to the
vnion of faith, with the Head therof, or to perfwade

E   an

*The infeli-
city of
Cruelty.*

*Q. Elizab.
her cruell
perfecutiós*

another to be a Catholicke , or do the same: When they read these things (I say) and many others, which for breuity I pretermitt, and that all this notwithstanding, she would not haue it said, *That she persecuted any for Religion* (which in manner this Apologer sticketh not to auouch) *nor put any Priest to death for that cause in deed*, wheras notwithstading she shed the bloud of aboue one hūdred and thirty , that might haue had their lyues euen at the last cast, if in this one point of Religion they would haue yielded neuer so little. All this (I say) being read and considered, seemeth vnto forreiners a strange infelicity both of body and soule.

XIII Especially when it is considered to what perpetuall iealosy at length she was brought vnto, of all sorts of people, *Puritans, Papists*, yea of her owne dearest, as the death of the Earle of *Essex*, and his followers, doth easily declare. Neyther was there any weeke lightly, but that she had some new teares, of some Priest or Iesuite, or Catholicke souldiours sent from *Flanders, France,* or *Italy* to kill her by violence, others from *Spayne* , and other Countryes to poyson her, or at at least, her * Chaire. And vpon such fancyes, men must be made away for greater terrour ; yea Iewes must be brought in also in this kynd of pretended poysoning, as the case of Doctor *Lopez* well declareth. Nay further this gryping passion of feare and iealosy did so vexe & consume her inwardly, as she was neuer well, vntill she had made away, against all law of Nature and Nations, the nearest vnto her in Royall bloud , that lyued vpon earth, and coequall with her in dignity, if in sundry respects not Superiour , I meane his Maties noble renowned *Mother* , Queene of *France* & *Scotland*, that by force of the former Statute, which declared this other for illegitimate and incapable of the Crowne (as now yow haue heard) should haue enioyed the Crowne of *England* presently after the death of *Q. Marie* , & consequently

* The fiction of *Squier* an. 1598.

Q. Eliz. her dealing towards her cosen of Scotland.

quently his Matie had enioyed the same 38. yeares at least, before he came vnto it after her death, who of all other lyuing Creatures, is knowne most hartily to haue hated that yssue & succession. And as she went about to disinable the same in the very roote & foūtayne it selfe, by seeking the disgrace of the ospring, by dishonour of the origen : so neuer ceased she afterward to continue practises against them both, vntill she had wracked the one, and brought the other also to great probability therof, if she might haue lyued to her will, or haue dyed with such vse of senses and iudgment, as might haue made way to her bad affections in that behalfe.

X I V. Well then, all this I haue beene inforced to speake vpon this occasion : first to represse somwhat therby the insultation of our foresaid Orator, in calling her, *The happy Queene, the blessed Queene, whose vnmatched wisedome, and vnconquered prowesse* (to vse his words) *crowned her the peerlesse wonder of her sexe.* All which tendeth to the exprobration of Catholicks, for hauing had so happy & peerles a persecutour; and to the insultation also ouer the Pope, for calling her in his *Breue*, as he saith, *Miseram Fœminam*, a miserable woman: which how true or false it is, I leaue to the prudent Reader out of the former discourse, about her byrth, youth, age and end, to censure.

Lo. Cooke in his Charge at Norwich. 4. August. 1606.

X V. Secondly I do heerin but imitate the first ancient Fathers, that wrote for defence of those holy Martyrs, that dyed for Christian Religion in the Primitiue Church, as namely, *Iustinus Martyr, Irenæus, Tertullian,* and others, who to comfort the afflicted, and to honour more their cause, did put them in mynd what manner of people their first persecutours were; as namely *Nero* and *Domitian,* what lyfe they led, what end they made, and the like; And that indeed they were fit instruments, to be the first, in such a worke. And the like we may say to Catholicks of *Q. Elizabeth,* that she

What māner of Persecutour Q. Elizabeth was.

E 2   being

being the strangest woman that euer was borne for diuers circumstances, now partly touched, and the first absolutly of that sexe, eyther Christian or created, that tooke vpon her Supreme power in Spirituall and Ecclesiasticall matters; it must needes be some comfort to Catholicke people, that God chose such an instrument to be their first scourge, out of all woman kynd.

XVI. And lastly, for that this Apologer will needs take vpon him, *to sacrifice to her* Manes: I thought my selfe obliged to offer some incense in like maner to the same, for mitigating the euill sent, which that notorious vntrue assertion must needs import, to the senses of all vnderstanding Readers: That, *Queene Elizabeth neuer punished any Papist for Religion, Nor made any rigorous law against them, before* Pius Quintus *his Excommunication, nor since that tyme, but vpon priuate plots, machinations, &c.* For cleare confutation wherof, I remit those of the elder sort that lyue in *England,* to their owne eyes, eares, and other externall senses, and those of yonger age, to the books of Statutes, of *Q. Elizabeths* tyme, *Iohn Stowes* Chronicle, and other such publicke Records. And so much of this poynt.

XVII. Next after these exaggerations *of the clemency and indulgence of Q. Elizabeth* towards Catholicks, this Apologer passeth on to bestow some of his adulation, and *oleum peccatoris,* vpon his Matie in like manner that now raigneth, telling vs, *That his kyndnes and benefits bestowed vpon that sort of people, haue bene farre greater then those of Q. Elizabeth;* which may easily be, as, by that, which hath bene touched, may appeare. Yet do we verily perswade our selues, that if his Highnes had byn left to himselfe, and to his owne Royall nature, and noble disposition in this poynt (as * *Q. Elizabeth* was wont to say of her disposition in religion) we had tasted, indeed, much of this his great humanity, and so we began, for some tyme: but being preuented and diuerted by the subtile workings of this, and other such Ministers, as desyred

* See Answer. to Syr Edward Cooke ca. 15.

syred to draw bloud, and to incite his Maieftie againft
vs, we hauing no place to fpeake for our felues, no admittance to be heard, no effectuall interceffour to interpofe his mediation for vs; no maruaile though wee
were caft of, and do indure the fmart.

XVIII. And I do name this Minifter (T. M. the
yonger) in the firft place among the reft, for that it is
commonly faid, that his whole exercife is Sycophancy
and calumniation againft men of our profeffion, be
they ftrangers, or domefticall: and that among other
deuifes, he hath this ; That euery tyme his Matie is to
take his repaft, he is ready, eyther with fome tale, ieft,
fcoffe, or other bitter lance to wound vs abfent, and that
he hath euer lightly, fome booke and page therof, ready
to read to his Highnes, fomewhat framed by his art to
incenfe or auert his Matie more, eyther in iudgement,
or affection, or both ; and therby to draw from him
fome hard fpeaches, which being publifhed afterward
by himfelfe, and others, do ferue to no other end, but to
gall and alienate myndes, and to afflict them, that are
not fuffered to giue reafon for themfelues. And that is
the feruice he doth his Matie in this exercife.

XIX. And as for the places themfelues, which he
vfeth to bring forth with his wet finger, as is faid, we
are to imagine, that they are no better, nor more fitly
applyed, then fuch as he hath fett forth againft vs in this
booke, & perhaps fomewhat worfe, for that he might
probably thinke, that this booke would be examined,
comming forth with fo great pretence of authority, as
it doth: And therfore if heere yow fynd him to vfe calumniation, & moft impertinent citation of Authours,
and Authorityes, eyther wholy making againft himfelfe, or nothing for his purpofe, or againft vs : then may
yow thinke what liberty he will take to himfelfe there
in fpeach, where no man is like to contradict him, but
all applaufe is expected from the ftanders by.

His Maie-
fties myld
difpofition
diuerted.

The exer-
cife of the
Minifter
Th. Mont.

XX. Let vs heare, if yow pleafe, one exaggeration of his, concerning his Maties myldnes vnto vs, and our ingratitude in abufing the fame to pryde. *His Ma.*^{ties}

Apol. pag.
18.

gouernment (faith he) ouer them hath fo far exceeded that of Q.
" *Elizabeth, in mercy and clemency, as the Papifts themfelues*
" *grew to that height of pryde, in confidence of his myldnes,*
", *as they did directly expect, and affuredly promife to them-*
", *felues liberty of Confcience, and equality with vs in all things,*
", *that are his ieft, and faithfull Subiects &c.* Do you fee what a height of pride this was? And what an abufe of his Maiefties mercie and clemencie, to expect libertie of Con-

Liberty of
Confciéce.

fcience? Why had he not obiected in like manner, that they expected the libertie of breathing, and vfing the common ayre, as well as Proteftants? For that neither breathing, nor the vfe of cómon ayre, is more due vnto them, or common to all, then ought to be libertie of Confcience to Chriftian men, wherby ech one liueth to God, and to himfelfe, and without which he ftrug-leth with the torment of a continuall lingring death.

XXI. And furely, I cannot but wonder, that this Minifter was not afhamed to call this the *height of pride*, which is generally found in all Proteftants neuer fo humble: yea the more humble, and vnderlings they are, the more earneft are they both in bookes, fpeaches, and preachings, to proue that liberty of Confcience is moft confórme to Gods law, and that wrefting, or for-cing of Confciences, is the higheft Tyranny, that can be exercifed vpon man. And this we may fee firft, in all M. *Fox* his Hiftory, efpecially during the time of the three King *Henries*, 4. 5. and 6. and afterward, when thofe that were called *Lollards*, and *Wickliffians*, who as M. *Fox* faith, were indeed good Proteftants, being preffed fomewhat about their Religion, did continu-ally beate vpon this argumét of libertie of Confcience, and when they obteyned it not, they fet vp publicke fchedles vpon the Church dores of *London*, and made
thofe

those famous conspiracyes of killing K. *Henry* the 5. and all his family, which are recounted by *VValsingham, Stow, Fox,* and other Englilh Hiltoriographers. *In vita Hērici quinti.*

XXII. In this our age alfo, the firlt oppofitiō of Proteltant Princes in *Germanie,* againlt their Emperour *Charles* the 5. both at *Smalcald, Aufiburgh,* and other meetings; as afterwards alfo the fierce and perillous warrs by the Duke of *Saxony, Marques* of *Brandeburge,* and other Proteltant Princes, and their people, againlt the fame Emperour, begunne in the very fame yeare that our K. *Henry* dyed. Were they not all for lyberty of Confcience? *Anno* 1546

lo, pretended, lo printed, lo publilhed, lo diuulged to the world? The firlt Supplications, Memorialls, and declarations in like manner, which the Protestants of *France* let forth in print: as alfo they of *Holland,* & *Zeland* Liberty of confcience demāuded by all Proteftants. in tyme of the gouernments, as well of the Duchesse of *Parma,* Duke of *Alua, Commendador Mayor,* and other Gouernours: did they not all exprelly protesse, that their principall griefes were, about liberty of Confcience reltrayned. And did not they cyte many places of *Scriptures,* to proue the equity & necelſity therof? And do not all Protestants the like at this day, in all places, where they are, both in *Polonia, Auftria, Hungaria, Bohemia, Styria,* and els where? And how the is *Iordanus conuerfus retrorfum,* with this Minilter? How is his voyce contrary to the voyce & fenfe of all the relt? How, & with what reafon, may he call it *the height of pryde* in Englilh Catholicks, to haue but hope therof, which is fo ordinary a doctrine & practice of all his brethren in forraine nations, to witt, for vs to expect liberty of Confcience, at the firlt entrance of our new King, of fo noble, and royall a mynd before that tyme, as he was neuer knowne to be giuen to cruelty, or perfecutiō in his former raigne? The Sonne of fuch a Mother, as held her felfe much beholden to Englilh Catholicks? And himfelfe in his litle *Golden* * *Βασιλι- κὸν Δῶρον.*

* *Booke* to his Sonne the Prince, had confelled that he

had

had euer found the Catholicke party moſt truſty vnto him, and therupon had done ſundry fauours to diuers of them, and gyuen no ſmall hope of greater vnto others?

XXIII. From this King (I ſay) whom they ſo much loued, and honoured, receyued ſo gladly, and with vniuerſall ioy, meant to ſerue faithfully; & truſted that as he had vnited the two Kingdomes in one Obedience by his Succeſſion : ſo would he by his liberality, vnite and conioyne the harts of all his Subiects, in bearing a ſweete and equall hand towards them all : From ſuch a King (I ſay) for vs to expect liberty of Conſcience, and equality with other Subiects (in this poynt at leaſt of freedome of ſoule) *what height of pryde* may it be called? May it not rather ſeeme *height of pryde* in this Miniſter, & his fellowes, that hauing byn old enemyes, and alwayes borne a hard, & hatefull hand, and tongue againſt his Ma.ᵗⁱᵉ both in their Sermons, Bookes, Speaches, all the tyme of the late Queenes raigne ; now vpon the ſuddayne *ſine vllis meritis præcedentibus*, will needs be ſo priuiledged, & aſſume vnto themſelues ſuch a confident preſumption of his Ma.ᵗⁱᵉˢ ſpeciall fauour, as to ſuffer no man to ſtand by them, but to hold it for *height of pryde* in vs, to hope for any freedome and liberty of our Conſcience at all? What is *height of pryde* and folly, if this be not?

XXIV. But his Ma.ᵗⁱᵉ is wiſe, & will, as we hope, according to his prudence, in tyme, looke into this ſort of men, and manner of proceeding. And to returne to the Apologer, he reckoneth vp (therby to exaggerate the more our ingratitude) the particuler fauours his Ma.ᵗⁱᵉ did vnto vs, at his firſt entrance, as, *That he did honour diuers Catholicks with Knighthood, being open Recuſants: That, he gaue audiēce indifferently to both ſydes: beſtowed equally fauours and honours vpon both profeſſions: gaue free con:inuall acceſſe to all rankes, and degrees of Papiſts in his Court and company: freeing*

                                          Recuſants

Height of pride, and in whome it may be ſaid to be.

Apol. pag. 19.

Recusantes from their ordinarie payments: gaue order to his Iudges with his owne mouth, to spare execution of all Priests, though they were conuicted: gaue libertie by his gracious Proclamation to all Priests not taken, to go out of the Countrey by such a day, and all Priestes that were taken, were sent ouer, and sett at liberty: and many other gracious fauours & benefittes: *VVhich* (saith he) *tyme and paper would fayle me if I would make enumeration of them all: in recounting wherof euery scrape of my pen* (to vse his words) *would serue but for a blott of the Popes ingratitude, and iniustice in meating his Ma.*tie *with so hard a measure for the same. So as I thinke* (quoth he) *I haue sufficiently wiped of the teares from the Popes eyes, for complayning vpon such persecution* &c.

Exprobra-
tion of his
Maiestyes
benefits
towards
Catholiks.

XXV. Thus writeth this man, who, in naming *the Popes ingratitude,* must much more include ours, that are Catholicks; for that these benefitts, such as they were, appertayned nothing to the *Pope*, but only in Christian charity, as a common spirituall Father and Pastour, he being otherwise a stranger vnto vs in bloud, and for other worldly respects. And as for Catholicks, they accept gratefully, whatsoeuer least fauour hath byn, or is done vnto them: and do not doubt, but that if his Ma.tie had not bene preuented by sinister information, & persuasion of others, they had tasted of much greater, as due vnto them, in that they are naturall borne Subiects of the Realme, most loyall in hart & affection, & neuer meaning otherwise, but to liue in most orderly and dutifull Subiection and Obedience to his Highnes, as to their liege Lord and Soueraigne.

Catholiks
dutifull
demea-
nour to his
Maiesty.

XXVI. And wheras this man, for proofe of the contrary, nameth the powder-treason of a few, therby to discredite the whole, though this calumniation haue beene answered before: yet now I ad further, as one said, *Distingue tempora, & scripturam concordabis,* If there had bene no persecution before that treason, this might haue beene assigned for some probable cause of

F the

the subsequent tribulations: but all *England* knoweth, that this is not so, but that his Maties sweete & myld aspect towards Catholicks at his first entrance, was soone, by art of their enemyes, auerted long before the conspiracy fell out. For that, not only all the most cruell Statutes and penall Lawes made by Q. *Elizabeth* were renewed and confirmed before this, with addition of others, tending to no lesse rigour & acerbitie : but also the exaction of the same was put in practice with great seueritie ; & namely the paymēt of the twenty poundes a moneth, or two partes of their goods and landes for Recusants (once remitted by his Matie as heere is confessed) were not only recalled againe : but the arrearages therof in like manner exacted ; and for leuying wherof, throughout sundry shyres of the Realme (especially in the North) there was such ransacking of mens houses, such dryuing away of their Cattell frō their groundes, such strayning of their Rents, such vexing of their tennants (not knowne perhaps to his Matie) as if the whole Countrey had byn gyuen ouer to spoyle & desolation.

Anno 1. *Iacobi Regis.*

XXVII. Nor were mens goods and persons only afflicted, but the lyues also of sundry taken away for cause of their Religion before this powder-treason fell out : which desperate treason, to ascribe as an effect and fruite of too much clemency in his Matie (as this Minister doth) is a strange assertion, no doubt : for so much, as such effects do not proceed, but of exasperated myndes ; which clemency worketh not, eyther in men or beasts. Neyther did euer any learned Philosopher, that wrote of the good institution of any Common wealth, or of the security of any Prince in his Gouernment, put such effects for fruits of clemency, but rather of the contrary manner of proceeding. And if all the disasterous ends of the most vnfortunate Princes, that euer haue byn destroyed, should be layd togeather, and the

Apol. pag. 19.

Clemency no cause of desperate attempts.

the caufes therof exactly inquired, it would be found fo: and confequently that this Minifter is no good Coun- fellour to his Ma.tie in this fo great & weighty affayre. And we hope that Almighty God, by the mercy of his deareft Sonne our Sauiour, and through the prayers of his Ma.ties good Mother, and other holy Princes of his Royall bloud now in heauen, will neuer fuffer him, at the egging of fuch exafperating people, to follow fo violent, troublefome, and dangerous a courfe, and fo contrary to theirs, whiles they lyued vpon earth, and fo alienate from his owne fweete nature and Princely difpofition.

XXVIII. But to proceed a litle further in the nar- ration of fome poyntes of heauy perfecutiõ, that inſued foone after his Ma.ties being in *England*, much before the powder-treafon was attempted : Who doth not know what afflictions were layd vpon Catholicks, euen in the very firft yeare of his Ma.ties raigne, efpe- cially towards the end therof, & much more through all out all the fecond yeare, before the faid powder-treafon fell out. For then not only in the Shires and Prouinces abroad : but euen in *London* it felfe, and in the eyes of the Court, the violence, and infolency of continuall fear- ches grew to be fuch, as was intollerable ; no night paffing commonly, but that Souldiours, & Catch-poles brake into quiet mens houfes, when they were afleepe, and not only carryed away their perfons vnto prifons at their pleafure, except they would brybe them excef- fiuely, but whatfoeuer liked them beft befydes in the houfe, eyther of Bookes, Cuppes, Chalices, or other fur- niture, that might any wayes feeme, or be pretended to belong to Religion, was taken for a prey, and feazed on. And among others, I remember, that one frend of myne, had a drinking Cuppe of fyluer taken from him, for that it had the name of I Es vs engrauen vpon it, though otherwife the forme therof did well fhew, that

(margin note:) The cru- elty of fe- arches.

F 2   it

it was but a Cuppe, & no Chalice. And thefe fearches
were made with fuch violence, and infolency, as diuers
gétlewomé were drawne or forced out of their beds,to
fee whether they had any facred thing,or matter belonging to the vfe of Catholick Religion, either about
them,or vnder their bedds.

XXIX. What fhall I fpeake of the cafting into
prifons, & condemnation to death of many Catholicks
for the fame caufe, in euery corner lightly of the Countrey, as namely in *London* of *M. Hill* the Prieft, and this
only for his function, and for comming into *England*
againft the Statutes of Queene *Elizabeth* to the contrary?
Of *M. Sugar* alfo an other Prieft in *VVaruicke*, that was

* *Anno*
1604. menfe
Auguſt.

not only condemned,but * executed withall rigour in
that Cittie for the fame caufe, and a lay man with him
named *Robert Gryfold*, for receyuing him into his houfe?
At *Oxford* alfo foure Priefts being taken at that tyme
whofe names were *M.Greene*, *Tichborne*, *Smith*, and *Brifco*,
all had fentence of death paffed vpon them;though atter
many afflictions fuffered in the pryfon there, which
made them defyre much the fpeedy execution of the
fentence gyuen againft them, they had infteed of this
one death, many deathes layd vpon them, by fending
them prifoners to the Caftle of *VVisbich*, where they
receyued fuch cruell vfage both in their diet,lodging &
other treatie, as made euen dyuers Proteftants to take
compaffion of them.And why was all this,but for their
Religion?

XXX. I let paffe the condemnation to death of a
poore man in Oxford named *Shitell*, for that the Prieft
M. Greene had fledde into his houfe,when he was purfued by the fearchers,through which condemnation,&
perpetuall imprifonment therupon enfuing, were
brought to extreme mifery & calamity, his poore wyfe
and children, moft lamentable to behold, or heare recounted. And vpon like occafion was apprehended,
impri-

imprifoned, condemned, & executed in *Yorke*, about the fame tyme, an other Lay-man named *Thomas VVylborne*, only for that he had vfed fome words of perfwafion to a certayne woman to be a Catholicke, notwithftanding the prohibition of her husband, who followed fo hoatly the matter againft him, as he caufed him to be put to death. I pretermit M.ʳⁱˢ *Shelley* a Gentlewoman of good Worfhipp, caft into the common Iayle at *VVorcefter* for that the Prieft M. *Haffells*, was found in her houfe. The apprehenfion in like manner, & condemning to death of M. *Edward Tempeft* Prieft and Gentlemā in London at the fame tyme. I paffe ouer the cruell fentence of cutting of the ears, of fo ancient & venerable a Gentlemam, as is M. *Tho. Pound*, that had lyued aboue thirty yeares in fundry prifons only for being a Catholicke, and now laft in his old age, had that honour from God, as to be fentenced to leefe his eares and ftand on the Pillorie in dyuers markets, for complayning of hard meafure, & iniuft execution, vfed againft Catholicks, contrary (as he prefumed) to his Ma.ᵗⁱᵉˢ intention.

Diuers examples of feuere perfecution.

XXXI. And fynally I paffe ouer what was practifed in *Herefordshire, Lancashire*, & other places in this kynd of perfecution, and particulerly concerning the new angariation and preffure, then firft brought vp, that men fhould be boūd to pay for their wyues, that were Recufats, a thing neuer before exacted in the former Queenes tyme. I pretermit alfo to métion, how his M.ᵗⁱᵉ before this, had reiected the cōmon, & humble fupplication of Catholicks, exhibited in writing for fome toleratiō, & mitigation of the calamityes: the which fupplication was anfwered with contépt & infultatiō by a Minifter, and put in print. His Ma.ᵗⁱᵉ in like manner had gyuen publike audience both to *Proteftants* & *Puritanes* for three dayes togeather, concerning the differences of their Religion: but to Catholicks he neuer yealded to gyue any at all. And how then can this Apologer talke fo

much

much of equality vfed in all fauours? How can he fay,
that there was no perfecution before the powder-
treafon?

XXXII. But let vs go forward yet fomewhat further: his Maieftie had before this tyme vpon other mens
importunity, confirmed, and ratified by his Letters
Patents, all that heape of Conftitutions, and Canons,
(being in number aboue an hundred & fourty) which
the BB. of *London* & *Canterbury*, had deuifed, & fet
forth againft Catholicks, for their greater vexation, &
affliction. Out of which hath flowed fince a huge fea
of moleftations and exagitations, by fearchings, fpoyles
citations, apprehenfions, excommunications, and other
violences, vpon innocent and quiet people, by the rauenous hungry Purfeuants of thofe Prelats, and other
their Catch-poles, without refpect, either of Iuftice, or
hope of remedy, for iniuryes by them offered. There had
paffed alfo before this, the fpeach of the *L. Chancelour* in
the Star-Chamber, and the Sermon of the B. of *London* at
Paules-Croffe, both of them tending to take all hope from
Catholicks of any leaft fauour, that might be expected,
and the former exprefly charging the Iudges in his
Maties name, to vfe all feuerity in feeking out and pu-
nifhing them. Which things being feene, and farre
worfe feared, yea defigned alfo and threatned, as thofe
Gentlemen apprehended it, (efpecially at the next Parlament) caft them into that wofull impatience, and precipitation, which the euent declared.

XXXIII. All this then which the Apologer heere
telleth vs, of Catholicks ingratitude for fo many benefits receyued, during his Maties raigne, and, *That it is a
mayne vntruth* (to vfe his words) *and can neuer be proued, that
any perfecution hath beene in his faid Maties gouernment, or that
any were, or are put to death or punifhed for caufe of Confcience*, is
fuch a kynd of fpeach, as if it were told in the *Indies*,
many thoufand myles of, where nothing is knowne of

our

The B. of
Londons
Sermon 5.
Auguft.
1605.

Apol. p.
21.

our Countryes affayres, might perhaps fynd some hearers that would belieue it : but in *England* to auouch such a thing in Print, where all mens outward senses, eyes & eares are witnesses of the cōtrary, is a strange boldnes. For as for persecution in goods and lands, as also of mens bodyes by imprisonment, and other vexations, who can deny the same, that will not shut his said eyes, or eares, from seing and hearing that which daylie passeth within the Realme. And when nothing els were: Yet those two seuerall and most memorable Statutes, to witt, the 4. and 5. made in the third yeare of this Kings raigne, conteyning more seuerall heads of affliction, and angariation against Catholicke-Recusants for their meere Conscience, then euer, perhaps, in the world were seene extant, against any one sorte of wicked men, or malefactors before; do easely conuince the vntruth of this asseueration about freedome from persecution. And as for death, which is lesse greiuous to many then those other persecutions, the late example of M. *Robert Drury*, and now againe these last monethes past, of M. *Matthew Flathers*, & M. *Geruis* Priestes (to omit others) that dyed expresly for refusing this late deuised Oath, since the powder-treason, cannot, I thinke, be answered, except he will say, that this *Oath* hath no matter of Conscience in it for a Catholicke man to receaue: the contrary wherof we haue euidently shewed before, by many demonstrations.

X X X I V. Wherfore, that which he addeth immediatly, insinuating, and expresly threatning, that as there hath beene no persecution, or putting to death before (which is not true as I haue shewed:) so now forsomuch as the Pope hath interposed his Authority, and forbidden the *Oath* as vnlawfull, there may chance be greater persecution, and more aboundant shedding of bloud, which (as he saith) must light vpon the Popes head, for this his prohibition: All this (I say) is so spoken

as

Increace of persecution since the pow-den-treason.

Statut. 4. & 5. *Anno* 3. *Iacobi Reg.*

Lond. 26. *Febr.* 1607. *York.* 21. *Mar.* 1608. *Lond.* 11. *Apr.* 1608.

Pag. 21. ,, ,, ,,

as ech man may fee, whither it tendeth: to witt, to in-
cyte his Matie by fuch deuifes, to ingulfe himfelfe into
the effufion of Catholickes bloud, cafting on the pretence, and veile of the Popes intermedling, as caufe therof: which is an ancient Art of deceipt, to giue *Non caufam,*
pro caufa: for that no iniury is euer offered vnder the
name of iniury, but of iuftice or merit . And our Sauiour was crucified as a deceyuer of the people, & difloyall

Luc. 23. *&*
Matth. vlt.
Act. 24.

to *Cæfar*:and *S. Paul* purfued as a difturber of the Weal-
publicke and peace. And no fuffering is fo honourable,
as that which commeth with a difhonourable title : fo
as Englifh Catholickes muft not be difmaied when
they fuffer for the falfe imputation of Ciuill Difloyal-
tie to their Temporall Prince, being witting to themfelues, that it is indeed for their Religion, and loyalty
to God, their eternall Prince, and fupreme King. And
this only fhall fuffice for this matter. For if Catholickes further affliction be determined by their Aduerfaries, and permitted by God, pretences will not want
how to do it. The prouerbe is already knowne, *Fa-*
cilè inuenies baculum , vt canem cadas, as alfo the fable of
Æfope, that the lambe muft be flayne, for that drinking
farre beneath the well, he was pretended notwithftanding, to haue troubled the fountaine . Catholicks muft
be beaten, for that the Pope hath refolued a cafe of
Confcience, that men may not fweare againft
their owne Religion . All be to the glory
of God, and then fynally will they
leefe nothing therby, which
is the only comfort in
fuch manner of
fufferings.

The

The second Part of this Paragraph.

 N E other poynt only is handled by the Apologer in this Paragraph, which is a large insultation against the *Pope*, for that he sayth in his *Breue*, as heere is alledged, *That the Oath cannot be taken with safety of the Catholicke faith, and of their soules health; since it conteyneth many things, that are* *Apol. pag. 21.*
playnly, & directly *contrary to their faith and saluation.* And albeit the word *(directly)* be conueyed in heere, which is not in the Popes Breue, & is of no small momēt, as all Deuines know in this matter, and therfore ought not to haue byn thrust in, as the Popes word, in a different distinct letter: yet not to stand vpon that, but vpon more grosser poyntes, and more iniurious, he presently vseth the speach, which is reported to haue byn of *Auerroes* the *Mahometan* Philosopher against *Moyses Lawgiuer* of the Iewes, *Multa dicit, sed pauca probat,* he saith much but proueth little, and presently passeth to this insultation, *How the naturall allegiance of Subiects to their Prince, can be directly opposite* (marke how he serueth himselfe of his owne word shifted into the text) *to the faith and saluation of soules, is farre beyond my simple reading in Deuinity, as I must* *Vixit An. 1150.*

Pag. 22.

G   *thinke*

it a strange and new assertion to proceed out of the mouth of that
pretended generall Pastour of Christian soules.

XXXVI. Heere now what abuse is offered to the
words and meaning of the *Breue*, euery simple Reader
will see, without any explication from me: for that
the Pope doth not prohibite naturall Obedience in
things lawfull; nor doth say, that such naturall, or cyuill
Obedience is opposite to faith or saluation of soules; nor

The Oath why it is vnlawfull.

that the Oath is vnlawfull, for exhibiting such naturall,
or cyuill Obedience: but for that, besydes this exaction
of naturall Obedience, which is lawfull, it conteyneth
diuers other poyntes also, concerning matters of Catholicke Religion: which poyntes being so conioyned,
and couched with the other, as the one cānot be sworne
without those other, do make the whole Oath vnlawfull, as it lyeth, without distinction, as before hath byn
declared. So as this charge is now proued, to be but a
meere cauill, and calumniation, & voluntary mistaking
of the question and controuersy in hand.

XXXVII. And yet doth he so insist in it, and so dila-
teth himselfe vpon this false surmised principle (*that*
Cyuill Obedience is denyed) as though all his Discourse and
Treatise depended only of this (as indeed it doth) and
therfore he entreth into the consutation therof with a
great florish of Scriptures, Fathers, and Councells
(wherin he and his do abound, when they say the same
that we do, but otherwise are altogether barren) as
though in earnest we did deny it: which thing neuer
so much as passed through our cogitations, but do hold
and teach that Subiects are bound to obey their Temporall Princes in all things lawfull, and those not only
good Princes, but bad also: and not only out of feare or
flattery, but out of Conscience, as the Apostle teacheth

Rom.13.

propter Conscientiam, for Conscience sake, but not *contra*
Conscientiam, against Conscience. Which being so; all is
meerly impertinent, that is alledged heere by the Apologer

loger, out of Scriptures, Fathers, and Councels, to proue,
that which we grant without proofe, & neuer denyed :
which is, that temporal Princes are duely to be obeyed
for Conscience sake, so long as they command nothing
against Conscience. But let them shew but one only
Authority, sentence, example or testimony out of any of
these three kind of witnesses, Scriptures, Fathers, or
Councells, that we must obey Princes against our Conscience, or Religion, and I will grant he sayth somewhat to the purpose, otherwise he doth but leese tyme,
and abuse his Reader in making him belieue, that he
saith somwhat when he saith nothing. Let vs examyne
therfore some of his examples if yow please.

    X X X V I I I. He alledgeth for examples out of the
Scriptures, That the children of *Israel* obeyed the King
of *Babylon*, as also they exhibited temporall Obedience
vnto King Pharao of *Egypt*; as in like manner to *Cyrus*
King of *Persia* : All which examples we grant to be
true, and could ad many more, both of the *Iewes*, and
Christians that lyued peaceably vnder Infidell Princes
in those dayes. But lett one example (as I said) be
brought forth, wherin they obeyed them in poynts
contrarie to their Conscience or Religion, and it shall
be sufficient. We read in the Prophesie of *Daniel*, that
those three famous Iewes, *Sidrach, Misach*, and *Abdenago*,
were most trustie vnto King *Nabuchodonosor* in temporall
affayres, and so much esteemed by him, as he made them
his vniuersall Gouernors ouer all the workes of the Re-
gion of *Babylon*, saith the *Scripture* : and yet when it came
to the poynt, that he would haue them for his honour
and pleasure, and vpon his commandement, adore the
golden *Statua*, which he had set vp ; they forsooke him
flatly, and said to him in the presence of all his Nobility assembled togeather, that they were not so much
as to answere him in that Commandement, nor would
they do, as he had appoynted them.

                    G 2   **XXXIX.**

*Apol. pag.
22.
Hier.27.12.
Exod.5.1.
Esdr.1.3.*

Dan.3.12.

No obe-
dience a-
gainst God
& a mans
Consciece.

XXXIX. The like in effect did the ancienter Iewes do with King *Pharao* of *Egypt* ; for that albeit in temporall affayres they obeyed him, euen in that tyme when he oppreſſed, and perſecuted them moſt : yet in that he would haue had them ſtay and ſacrifice in *Egypt*, and not follow *Moyſes* their Spirituall Superiour into the deſert (notwithſtanding that the King had ſome cauſe perhaps to ſuſpect their temporall Allegiance, alſo by that departure, they being a potent multitude of people :) yet would they not obey him, nor do as he would haue them, when they perſuaded themſelues that God would haue the contrary.

Dan. 1.
Tob. 1.

XL. I lett paſſe how *Daniel* and his fellowes would not eate the meates of the King of *Babylon*, nor *Tobie* thoſe of the *Aſſyrians*, & much leſſe would he leaue of to bury the dead, though it were forbidden by Proclamation vnder payne of death, The *Machabees* in like manner obeyed King *Antiochus* ſo long, as he commanded nothing againſt their Law and Conſcience : but when he went about to force them to ſacrifice, and to eate ſwynes-fleſh, and other things againſt their Law and Conſcience, they refuſed openly to performe that Obedience. So as theſe places of Scriptures alledged by the Apologer, do proue nothing for him at all, but are rather flatt againſt him, and for vs, as yow haue ſeene.

1.Macha. 1.

Authorityes of aũcient Fathers.

XLI. And much more do make againſt him, his Authorityes alledged out of the ancient Fathers, for that they go about to proue the very ſame poynt that we heere hold, that in temporall & cyuill affayres we muſt obey dutifully our temporall Princes, though Infidels or Pagans : but not in matters concerning God, our Religion, or Conſcience. And his very firſt example out of *S. Auguſtine* is ſuch, as I maruaile much, that he would cyte the ſame, but that ſomwhat for ſhew muſt be alleadged : For it maketh ſo clearly & directly againſt
him.

him, as if it had beene written purposely to confute him in this our cafe. But let vs heare what it is. Agreable to the Scriptures (*saith he*) did the Fathers teach. *Auguſtine* speaking of *Iulian*, faith thus: *Iulian* was an vnbelieuing Emperour, was he not an *Apoſtata*? an oppreſſor, and an Idolatour? Chriſtiã fouldiours ferued that vnbelieuing Emperour: when they came to the caufe of Chriſt, they would acknowledge no Lord, but him that is in heauen: when he would haue them worſhip Idolls & facrifice, they preferred God before him: but when he faid, go forth to fight, inuade fuch a nation, they prefently obeyed: they diſtinguiſhed their eternall Lord from their temporall, and yet were they fubieĉt euen vnto their temporall Lord, for his fake, that was their eternall Lord and Maiſter. Thus he.

Apol. pag. 23. *Auguſt. in Pſal.* 124. ,, ,, ,, ,, ,, ,, ,,

XLII. And can any thing be fpoken more cleerly for vs, and for our caufe, then this? For euen thus do we offer to our King & Soueraigne: we will ferue him: we will obey him: we will go to warre with him: we will fight for him: and we will do all other offices belonging to temporall duty: but when the caufe of Chriſt commeth in hand, who is Lord of our Confciences, or any matter concerning the fame, or our Religion; there we do, as *S. Auguſtine* heere appoynteth vs, preferre our eternall King, before our Temporall.

,, How farre we are bound to our tēporall Prince.

XLIII. And like to thefe are all the other places of Fathers cyted by him, who diſtinguiſh expreſly betweene the Temporall honour and Allegiance due to the Emperour, and the other of our Religion, & Confcience, belonging only to God. And to that playne fenfe are *Tertullians* words cyted by the Apologer: *VVe honour the Emperour in fuch forte, as is lawfull for vs, and expedient for him, as a man fecond after God, and as hauing receyued from God, whatfoeuer he is, and only leſſe then God.* And will not the Catholicks of *England* vfe this fpeach alfo vnto their King Or will the Apologer himfelfe deny that *Tertullian*

Apol. pag. 23. *Tertull. ad Scap.*

G 3   heere

heere meant nothing els, but in temporall affayres, for much as the Emperours at that tyme were Heathen & Gentils, and consequently were not to be obeyed in any poynt againſt Chriſtian faith or Religion?

XLIV. The like playne doctrine haue the words of *Iuſtinus Martyr* to the Emperour himſelfe, cyted heere in the third place, to witt : *VVe only adore God, and in all other things wee cheerfully performe ſeruice to yow, profeſſing yow to be Emperours, and Princes of men.* And do not all Engliſh Catholiks ſay the ſame at this day, that in all other things, that concerne not God & his Obedience, by rule of Catholicke Religion, they offer cheerfully to ſerue his Matie , acknowledging him to be their liege Lord and King, & inferiour only to god in his Temporall Gouernment? And how then are theſe, and ſuch other places brought in for witneſſe, as though they had ſomwhat to ſay againſt vs?

XLV. The other two ſentéces, in like manner cyted out of *Optatus*, and *S. Ambroſe*, the firſt ſaying : *That ouer the Emperour there is none , but only God , that made the Emperour.* And the other, *That teares were his weapons againſt the armes, & ſouldiours of the Emperours : That he neyther ought , or could reſiſt* : Neyther of them do make any thing againſt vs , or for the Apologer , euen as they are heere nakedly cyted , without declaration of the circumſtances: for that in temporall affayres the King or Emperour is Supreme, next vnder God. And when the Emperour will vſe ſecular forces againſt the Prieſts of his dominion, they, being no ſouldiours, muſt fall to prayers, and teares, which are Prieſtly weapons. But what? Did *S. Ambroſe* by this acknowledge that the Emperour had higher Authority, then he, in Churchmatters? Or that if he had offered him an Oath, repugnant to his Religion, or Conſcience, in thoſe matters he would haue obeyed, or acknowledged his Superiority? No truly. For in three ſeuerall occaſions that fell

out

*Iuſt. Apol.
2. ad Anto.
Imperat.*

*Optat. cõtra
Parmen. li.
3. Ambroſ.
Orat. cõtra
Auxent. de
Baſilicis nõ
trad. lib. 5.
Epiſt.*

out, he flatly denyed the same, which this Apologer craftily dissembleth, and saith not a word therof.

XLVI. The first was, when he was cited by *Dalmatius* the Tribune, bringing with him a publicke Notarie to testifie the same, in the name of the Emperour *Valentinian* the yonger, to come and conferre, or dispute with the hereticall Bishop *Auxentius*, in the presence of his Matie and other of his Nobility and Counsell, which poynt S. *Ambrose* refused vtterly to do, tellyng the Emperour playnly by a letter, written vnto him; *That in matters of faith and Religion Bishops must iudge of Emperours, and not Emperours of Bishops.* And dyuers other doctrines, by this occasion, he taught him to that effect, as is to be seene in the same Epistle.

XLVII. The second occasion fell out the very next yeare after in *Milane*, when the said Emperour, by suite of the *Arrians*, and fauour of *Iustina* the Empresse on their behalfe, made a Decree that a certayne Church of that Citty should be deliuered to the said *Arrians* : which Decree S.*Ambrose* the Bishop refused to obey. And when the Emperours Officers comming with armes, vrged greatly to giue possession of the Church, he fled to his former weapons of weeping and praying: *Ego Missam facere cæpi &c.* I began to say Masse, and when the teporall Magistrate vrged still, that the Emperour vsed but his owne right, in appoynting that Church to be deliuered, S.*Ambrose* answered, *Quæ diuina sunt, Imperatoriæ Potestati non esse subiecta :* That such things as belonge to God, are not subiect to the Imperiall power. And thus answered S. *Ambrose* about the gyuing vp of a materiall Church. What would he haue said in greater matters.

XLVIII. The third occasion was, when the Emperour sent his *Tribunes*, and other Officers to require certayne Vessells belonging to the Church to be deliuered, which S.*Ambrose* constantly denyed to do, saying: *That in this, he could not obey :* And further adding,

That

Amb. Ibid.

Ambrof.
Concion. de
Basilicis nõ
tradendis
hær.to. 5.

,,

,,

,,

,,

That if the Emperour did loue him felfe, he should abftayne from offering fuch iniury vnto Chrift. And in another place, handling the fame more at large, he faith : That he gaue to Cefar that which was Cefars, and to God that which belonged to God : but that the Temple of God could not be the right of Cefar, which we fpeake (faith he) to the Emperours honour. For what is more honourable vnto him, then that he being an Emperour, be called a Child of the Church, for that a good Emperour is within the Church, but not aboue the Church. So *S. Ambrofe.* What would he haue done, or faid, if he had bene preffed with an Oath againft his Confcience, or any leaft poynt of his Religion ?

I L. Neyther doth the laft place cyted out of *S. Gregorie* the *Great* to the Emperour *Mauritius* make any thing more for our Apologers purpofe of taking Oathes againft Confcience. For albeit the fame Father do greatly complayne in dyuers places of the oppreffion of the Church by the Kingly power of *Mauritius,* whome (though otherwife a Catholicke Emperour) he compareth in that poynt to Nero and *Dioclefian,* faying : *Quid Nero ? quid Dioclefianus ? quid denique ifte, qui hoc tepore Ecclefiam perfequitur ? Nunquid non omnes portæ Inferi ?* What was *Nero ?* what was Dioclefian ? what is he who at this tyme, doth perfecute the Church ? Are they not all gates of Hell ? Yet in this place alledged by the Apologer, he yealded to publifh & fend abroad into diuers Countryes and Prouinces, a certayne vniuft law of the faid Emperours, that prohibited Souldiours, and fuch as had byn imployed in matters of publike accõpts of the Commõ Wealth, to make themfelues Monkes : which law, though *S. Gregorie* did greatly miflike, and wrote fharply againft it, to the Emperour himfelfe : yet to fhew his due refpect in temporall things vnto him, and for that indeed the law was not abfolutly fo euill, but that in fome good fenfe, it might be tolerated, to witt,
that

Apol. pag.
24.

How S.
Gregory a-
greed to
the pub-
lifhing of
the law of
the Empe-
rour *Mau-*
ritius.

Greg. lib.2.
Epiftol. 65.
Indict.11.

that Soldiours sworne to the Emperors warres, might not (during the said Oath & obligatiō) be receaued into Monasteryes, but with the Princes licence: yet for that it tended to the abridgment of Ecclesiasticall freedome, in taking that course or state of lyfe, which ech man chooseth for the good of his soule; *S. Gregorie* misliked the same, and dealt earnestly with the Emperour to relinquish it, or to suffer it to be so moderated, as it might stand without preiudice of Christian liberty: wherunto the Emperour at length yealded, and so *S. Gregorie* sent the same abroad vnto diuers Primates and Archbishoppes of sundry Kingdomes mencioned by him, but corrected first and reduced by himself, as supreme Pastour, to a reasonable lawfulnes, and temperate moderation: to witt, That those who had borne offices of charge in the Common wealth, and after desyred to be admitted to Religious life in Monasteryes, should not be receyued, vntill they had gyuen vp their full accompts, & had obteyned publicke discharge for the same. And that soldiours which demanded the like admittance, should be exactly tryed, and not admitted vnto Monasticall habite, but after they had lyued three yeares in their lay apparell, vnder probation.

L. This determineth *S. Gregorie* in his Epistle, beginning, *Gregorius Eusebio Thessalonicensi, Vrbicio Dirachitano, &c.* adding further in the same Epistle, as hath byn said, *De qua re, Serenissimus & Christianissimus Imperator omnimodò placatur:* About which matter our most Clement and Christian Emperour is wholy pleased and content. So as in this *S. Gregorie* shewed his pastorall care and power, in limiting and moderating the Emperours law, according to the law of God, though in temporall respectes he shewed him the Obedience, that was due vnto him. But what is this vnto our Oath? May we thinke that *S. Gregory*, that would not passe a temporall

Greg. lib. 7.
Epist. 11.
Indict. 1.

H law

law of the Emperour, without reprehenſion of the vnlawfulnes therof to the Emperour himſelfe, and cor-
rection therof in the publication, for that indirectly it
did infringe the liberty of Religious life , when men
were called therunto, that he would not haue much
more reſiſted the admiſſion of an Oath, about ſuch
affayres, if it had beene propoſed ? No man , I thinke,
in reaſon can imagine the contrary.

L I. The laſt thing thē that is cited without purpoſe
by this Apologer, are certayne Councels, which are ſaid
to haue ſubmitted themſelues to Emperours, as that of
Arles in *France* vnto *Charles* the Great their King: or that
in the laſt wordes of the ſaid Councell, the Biſhopps
there gathered togeather preſenting the ſame to the
ſame *Charles* write thus : *Hæc ſub breuitate , quæ emendatione*

Conc. Arel.
ſub Carol.
Can. 26.

digna perſpeximus, &c. Theſe things briefly which we
haue ſeene worthy of reformation, wee haue noted &
deemed to be preſented to our Lord the Emperour , be-
ſeeching his Clemency if any thing be wanting to ſup-
ply it by his wyſedome ; and if any thing be otherwiſe
done then reaſon requireth , it be amended by his iudgement; and if any thing be reaſonably cenſured, it may
be perfected by his helpe, and by the Clemency of Almighty God. *So the Councell.* And heerof would the Apologer inferre that this Councell of Biſhops ſubmitted it
ſelfe to the Emperour.

L I I. But I would aske him wherin? To take any
Oath that the Emperour *Charles* ſhould propoſe vnto
them ? Wee ſee no *Oath* offered, nor mentioned , and ſo
nothing heere to our purpoſe. Wherin then, or why are
they ſaid to haue ſubmitted themſelues ? For that, perhaps, it is ſaid in the Preface of the Councell, that they
were gathered togeather by order, and commandement
of the ſaid Emperour. Surely it was hard, that ſo many
Biſhops, & Archbiſhops ſhould be aſſembled togeather
without his liking, and Order. But that the conſent,
direction

direction, and chiefe Commiſſion for the ſame, came from the Biſhop of *Rome*, may eaſily be gathered: for that in the firſt Councell that he cauſed to be celebrated in his Dominions, which was that of *VVormes* in the yeare of Chriſt 770. it was left regiſtred in theſe wordes: *Auctoritas Eccleſiaſtica, atque Canonica docet, non debere, abſque ſententia Romani Pontificis, Concilia celebrari.* Eccleſiaſticall and Canonicall Authority teacheth, that Councels may not be held, without the allowance of the Biſhop of *Rome.*

LIII. And wherin thē? Or why is this ſubmiſſion made? For approbation of matters cōcerning faith? No, for that yow haue heard before out of *S. Ambroſe*, that therin Emperours are not iudges of Biſhops, but Biſhops of Emperours. Wherin then, or why is this ſubmiſſion, or rather remiſſion to the Emperour, and his iudgmēt? It was, for that this Councell was made onely for reformation of manners and matters, at the religious inſtāce of the good Emperour, the effectuating wherof did depend principally of his good will and aſſiſtance, and ſo after the firſt Canon, where briefly is ſet downe the Confeſſion of the Chriſtian faith, all the other 25. Canons (for there are only 26. in all) are about reformation of matters amiſſe: as for more diligence in daylie prayer for the Emperours perſon, and his children, to wit, that a *Maſſes and Litanies be ſaid daylie for them, by all Biſhops, Abbots, Monks, and Prieſts.* b That Biſhops and Prieſts ſtudy more diligently, and teach the people, both by leſſons and preachings: c That lay men may not put out Prieſts of their benefices, without the ſentence of the Biſhop, nor that they take money of them for collation of the ſaid benefices: d That none be admitted to enter into the Monaſteryes of Virgins, eyther to ſay Maſſe, or otherwiſe, but ſuch as be of approued vertue: e How peace is to be held betweene Biſhops, Earles, and other Great men, eſpecially in execution of Iuſtice: f That

weightes

Vide in Capitularibus Franc. li.6. c. 285. de Concilio VVormac.

Wherein the Councell of Arles did ſubmit it ſelfe to the Emperour.

a *Can.* 2.
b *Can.* 3.
c *Can.* 4.

d *Can.* 7.& 8.
e *Can.* 13.
f *Can.* 15.& 16.

g *Can.* 20.
22.23.

weightes and meafures be iuſt and equall, and that none worke vpon holy dayes : g That all Tythes be payd, all ancient poſſeſſions mantayned to the Churches : That no ſecular courtes be held in Churches, or Church porches : That no Earles, or other Great men do fraudulently buy poore mens goodes, &c.

LIV. Theſe then were the pointes of Reformation, decreed in that Councell of *Arles*, at the inſtance of *Charles* the *Great*, who was ſo zealous a Prince in this behalfe, as he cauſed fiue ſeuerall Councells to be celebrated in diuers Partes of his Dominions, within one yeare, to wit, this of *Arles*, an other at *Towers*, a third at *Chalons*, a fourth at *Mentz*, the fifth at *Rhemes*, and another the yeare before (which was the ſixt) *Ad Theodonis Villam*, which is a towne in *Luxemburge*. All which Prouinciall *Synodes* are extant in the third Tome of Coũcells, togeather, with the Canons and Decrees, which are ſuch as could not be put in execution, but by the temporall fauour, authoritie, and approbation of the Emperour in ſuch matters, as concerned his temporall Kingdome and iuriſdiction. Wherfore if for theſe reſpects, the Councell did preſent vnto the Emperour theſe Canons to be cõſidered of by his wiſedome, whether any thing were to be added, altered, or taken away, for the publicke good of the Common Wealth (no Controuerſy of faith being treated therin) what is this to proue, eyther, that the Emperour in ſpirituall matters was ſuperiour to the ſaid Biſhops, or that if he had propoſed vnto them any ſuch *Oath*, as this is, wherin by profeſſing their temporall Allegiance, they muſt alſo haue impugned ſome poynt of their faith, that they would haue obeyed him? And ſo much of this Councell.

LV. And for that, all the other Authorityes of other Councels heere cyted, do tend only to this end of prouing Temporall Obedience, which we deny not, but

do.

The zeale
of Charles
the Great
to haue
manners
reformed
by the au-
thority of
Biſhops.

do offer the same most willingly: we shall not stand
to answere or examine any more of them, but shall
end this Paragraph, with laying downe the insultation of this Apologer against the Pope, vpō his owne
voluntary mistaking the Question. I read (*sayth he*) in
the Scriptures, that Christ said, *His Kingdome was not of
this world*, bidding vs to giue to Cesar that which
was Cesars, and to God that which was Gods: and I
euer held it for an infallible Maxime in Deuinity, That
temporall Obedience to a temporall Magistrate, did nothing repugne to matters of faith or saluation of soules.
But that euer Temporall Obedience was against faith
and saluation of soules, as in this Breue is alledged, was
neuer before heard or read of in the Christian Church;
and therfore, I would haue wished the *Pope*, before he
had set downe this Commandement to all Papists
heere, That since in him is the Power, by the in-
fallibility of his spirit, to make new Articles of
faith, when euer it shall please him; That he had
first set it downe for an Article of faith, before he
had commanded all Catholicks to belieue, and obey it.
So he.

L V I. And I maruaile, that a man professing
learning, would euer so trysle, or rather wrangle, and
wrongfully charge his Aduersary: for that I fynde no
such thing in the *Breue* at all, as that Temporall Obedience is against faith and saluation of soules: nor
doth the *Breue* forbid it: nor doth any learned Catholicke affirme, that the Pope hath power *to make new Articles of Faith*: nay rather it is the full consent of all Catholicke Deuines, that the Pope, and all the Church togeather, cannot make any one new Article of beliefe,
that was not truth before, though they may explane
what points are to be held for matters of faith, & what
not, vpon any new heresies or doubts arising: Which
articles so declared, though they be more particulerly,

H 3   and

Margin notes:

Ioan. 18. 36.
Mat. 22. 21.
Apol. pag.
26. *&* 27.

,,
,,
,,
,,
,,
,,
,,
,,
,,
,,
,,
,,

Neither
the Pope
or Church
can make
any new
Articles of
Faith.

and perspicuously knowne now for points of faith, and so to be belieued, after the declaration of the Church then before: yet had they before the selfsame truth in themselues, that now they haue. Nor hath the said Church added any thing to them, but this declaration only. As for example, when *Salomon* declared the true Mother of the child that was in doubt, he made her not the true mother thereby, nor added any thing to the truth of her being the mother: but only the declaration. Wherefore this also of ascribing power to the Pope of *making new Articles of faith*, is a meere calumniation amongst the rest.

LVII. There followeth his conclusion: I will then conclude(saith he) my answere to this point in a Dilemma: Eyther it is lawfull to obey the Soueraigne in temporall things or not. If it be lawfull, as I neuer heard or read it doubted of: then why is the Pope so vniust and cruell towards his owne Catholicks, as to commaund them to disobey their Soueraignes lawfull commandement? If it be vnlawfull, why hath he not expressed any one cause or reason therof? But this *Dilemma* is easily dissolued, or rather falleth of it self, both his pillers being but broken reeds, framed out of false suppositions: For that the Pope neyther denyeth it, to be lawfull, to obey the Soueraigne in Cyuill and Temporall things: nor doth he command Catholicks to disobey their Prince his lawfull commádements: but only where they be vnlawful to be performed, as he supposeth them to be in the taking of this *Oath*. Wherof he expresseth sundry causes, and reasons, I meane, so many as the Oath it self cóteyneth points cócerning Religion: to which end, he setteth downe the whole Oath, as it lyeth, with intimation, that those points cannot be sworne with integrity of Catholicke Religion, & good conscience: which is sufficient for a Iudge, who disputeth not, but determineth. So as, hereupon to make
illa-

3. Reg. 3.

Wilfull mistaking of the controuersy.

illation of the Popes vniuſt, and cruell dealing towards Catholicks, by this his deciſion, as though he forbad Ciuill Obedience; is to buyld vpon a voluntary falſe ground, ſuppoſing, or rather impoſing the Pope to ſay, that which he doth not, and then to refute him, as though he had ſaid it indeed. And is this good dealing?

L V I I I. But yet he goeth forward vpon the ſame falſe ground to buyld more accuſations againſt the Pope, ſaying: That if the foundation of his exhorting Catholicks to beare patiently their tribulations, be falſe (*as this Apologer auoucheth it to be*) then it can worke no other effect, then to make him guylty of the bloud of ſo many of his ſheep, whome he doth thus willfully caſt away, not only to the needles loſſe of their liues, and ruyne of their famylies: but euen to the laying on of a perpetuall ſlander vpon all Papiſts. As if no zealous Papiſt could be a true Subiect to his Prince: and that Religion, and the Temporall Obedience to the Ciuill Magiſtrate, were two things incompatible and repugnant in themſelues. *Thus he.*

L I X. But who doth not ſee that theſe be all iniurious inferences, inforced vpon the former falſe ſuppoſitions, to witt, That Catholicks ſuffer nothing for their Conſcience, That there is no perſecution at all in *England*, That there is nothing exacted by this laſt oath, but *only* and *meerly* Ciuill Obedience, and that in this, the Pope exhorteth them to diſobey the Temporall Prince in Temporall dutyes, and thereby giueth iuſt occaſion to the Prince to vſe his ſword againſt them, and conſequently that he is cauſe of the effuſion of their bloud, and of the infamy of Catholicke Religion: as though no Catholicke by his Religion could be a true Subiect to his Temporall Prince. All which ſuppoſitions being vtterly miſtaken, and not true, the more often they are repeated, the more exorbitant ſeemeth

the

See S. Cyprian Exhort. ad Martyr.

the ouerſight of the wryter. And in my opinion, the very ſame might haue bene obiected vnto *S. Cyprian* and other Fathers of the Primitiue Church, that they were guylty of ſo many Martyrs bloud, willfully caſt away, and of the ruyne of their familyes, and other inconueniences, by exhorting them not to doe againſt their Conſciences, nor to yield to their Temporall Princes Commandements againſt God and their Religion: no not for any torments that might be layd vpon them, nor for any loſſes that might fall vnto them, of goods, life, honour, fame, friendes, wife, children, or the like, which were ordinary exhortations in thoſe daies of perſecution, as by their Bookes yet extant doth appeare.

L X. Neyther is it ſufficient to ſay, that thoſe tymes and ours are different, for that the things then demaunded were apparantly vnlawfull, but theſe not : for that, to vs that are Catholicks, theſe things are as vnlawfull now, as thoſe other were then to them, for that they are no leſſe againſt our Conſciences in matters of Religion. For why ſhould it be more damnable then, and indiſpenſable to deliuer vp a Byble, or new Teſtament, for examples ſake, when the Emperour commaunded it, then now to ſweare an Oath againſt our Conſcience and Religion, when our Temporall Prince exacteth it ? For that this, perhaps, is called the Oath of Allegiance ? Who knoweth not, that the fayreſt tytle is put vpon the fowleſt matter, when it is to be perſuaded or exacted ? And he that ſhall read the Hiſtoryes of that tyme, and of thoſe auncient afflictions, ſhall ſee that Act alſo to haue beene required, as of Obedience and Allegiance, and not of Religion, being only the deliuery vp of materiall bookes: and yet did the whole Church of God condemne them for it, that deliuered the ſame, and held

See Euſeb. lib. 8. ca. 4. & Aug. de Bap. lib. 7. cap. 2. &

held for true Martyrs, all thofe that dyed for denying thereof, for that they would not doe an Act againft their Confciences.

L X I. Well then, to draw to an end of this fecond paragraph about the two Breues of *Paulus Quintus*, two things more writeth this Apologer, whereunto I muit in like manner fay fomewhat. The firft is, That Pope *Clemens Octauus* fent into *England*, two Breues immediatly before the late Queenes death, for debarring of his Maieftie, our now Soueraigne, of the Crowne, or any other, that eyther would pro cffe, or any way tolerate the profefſurs of our Religion, contrary (faieth he) to his manifold vowes, and proteftations, *fimul & eodem tempore*, and, as it were, deliuered, *vno & eodem Spiritu*, to diuers of his Maieftyes Minifters abroade, pro effing all kyndenes, and fhewing all forwardnes to aduance him to this Crowne, &c. Wherein ftill I fynde the fame veyne of exaggeration, and calumniation continued by the Apologer. For hauing procured fome knowledge of thofe two Breues, I fynde them not fent into *England* togeather, *nor immediatly before the late Queenes death*, but the one diuers yeares before fhee dyed, and the other after her death, and this to different effects. For in the firft, the Pope being confulted, what Catholicks were bound to doe in confcience, for admitting a new Prince after the Queene fhould be dead, for fo much as fome of different Religions, were, or might be, pretenders; he determined that a Catholicke was to be preferred, not thinking (as may be prefumed) to preiudice therein his Maiefty that now is, of whome, vpon the relations, and earneft affeuerations of thofe his Maieftyes Minifters abroad, who heere are mentioned, he had conceaued firme hope, that his Highnes was not farre from being a

I   Catho-

lib.7. côtra Crefc. cap. 27. & Arnob. côtra Gentes lib. 4. in fine.

,,
,,
,,
,,
,,
,,
,,
,,
,,

Touching the two Breues of Clemens octauus. Anno Domini 1600. & 1603.

Catholicke, or at leaft wife not altogeather fo alienate from that Religion, or profeffours therof, as
reafonable hope might not be conceaued of his
conuerfion : though in regard of not preiudicing
his Tytle in *England*, the faid Minifters auouched,
that it was not thought expedient at that tyme to
make declaration therof.

LXII. This was auerred then, how truly
or falfly I know not. But many letters and tefti-
fications are extant hereof, which were the caufe
of thofe demonftrations of *Clemens Octauus*, to fauour
his M.^ties Tytle, which he did fo hartily and
effectually, as when he, after the Queenes death,
vnderftood that he was called for into *England*, he
wrote prefently the fecond Breue, exhorting all
Catholicks to receaue and obey him willingly, hoping that at leaftwife they fhould be permitted to
liue peaceably vnder him. And this is the very
truth of thofe two Breues : nor was there in the
former any one word againft his Maiefty then of
Scotland; and much leffe that he was therin called the
Scottifh Hereticke, as *Syr Edward Cooke* hath deuifed
fince, and falfely vttered in print without fhame
or confcience. Nor was there any fuch wordes, as
heere are alleadged, againft any that would but
tolerate the Profeffours of Proteftants Religion : nor was
there any fuch double dealing or diffimulation in
Pope Clement his fpeaches, or doings, concerning
his Ma.^ty as heere are fet downe. But the truth is,
that he loued his perfon moft hartily, and alwaies
fpake honourably of him, treated kindely all thofe
of his nation, that faid they came from him, or
any wayes belonged vnto him : and oftentymes vfed
more liberality that way, vpon diuers occafions,
then is conuenient, perhaps, for me to vtter
heere : caufed fpeciall prayer to be made for his
Maiefty,

In his
Charge at
Norwich
4. Auguft.
anno 1606.

Maiefty, wherof, I fuppofe, his Highnes cannot altogeather be ignorant, and much leffe can fo noble a nature be ingrate for the fame, which affureth me, that thofe things vtterd by this Apologer, fo farre from the truth, could not be conferred with his Maiefty, but vttered by the Authour therof, vpon his owne fplene, againft the Pope, and fuch as are of his Religion.

LXIII. The fecond and laft point affirmed by the Apologer in this Paragraph, is, that the firft of thefe two Breues of *Paulus Quintus* was iudged to be farre *againft Deuinity, Policy, and naturall fenfe, by fundry Catholicks, not of the fimpler fort, but of the beft account both for learning and experience among them, wherof the Archprieft was one, and confequently, that it was held but for a counterfaite libell, deuifed in hatred of the Pope.* &c. All this (I fay) hath much calumniation in it, and litle truth. For albeit fome might doubt, perhaps, whether it came immediatly from the Pope, *Ex motu proprio,* or only from the Congregation of the Inquifition, vpon defectuous information of the State of the queftion in *England* (of which doubt, notwithftanding, if any were, there could be little ground:) yet no Catholicke of iudgement or piety, would euer paffe fo farre, as to iudge it contrary *to Deuinity, Policy, or naturall fenfe,* and much leffe, *to be a libell deuifed in hatred of the Pope.* Thefe are but deuifes of the Minifter-Apologer: and he offereth much iniury to fo Reuerend a man as the Archprieft is, to name him in fo odious a matter, but that his end therin is well knowne. And if there were any fuch doubt, or might be before, of the lawfulnes of the firft Breue, now is the matter cleered by the fecond; and fo all men fee thereby, what is the fentence of the Sea Apoftolicke therein, which is fufficient for Catholicke men, that haue learned

To the laft poynt.

I 2   to

to obey , and to fubmitt their iudgements to
thofe , whome God hath appointed for the declaration, and decifion of fuch doubts. And thus much
about thofe two Breues. Now let vs fee
what is faid to *Cardinall Bellarmyne*,
for writing to M.*Blackwell*
in this affaire.

ABOVT

ABOVT
CARDINALL
BELLARMINES LETTER
TO Mr BLACKVVELL:
And answere giuen thereunto,
by the Apologer.

Paragr. III.

HE laſt Part of this Apology con-
cerneth a letter written by *Cardinall
Bellarmine* in *Rome*, vnto *George Blackwell* Arch-prieſt in *England*: which
letter, as appeareth by the argument
therof, was written out of this occaſion: That wheras vpon the comming forth of the forenamed new
Oath, intituled, *Of Allegiance*, there were found diuers
poynts combined togeather, ſome appertayning mani-
feſtly to Ciuill Allegiance, wherat no man made ſcruple, ſome other ſeeming to include other matters, contrary to ſome part of the Catholicke faith, at leaſt in
the common ſenſe as they ly ; there aroſe a doubt
whether the ſaid *Oath* might be taken ſimply and
wholy, by a Catholicke man, as it is there propoſed

*Apolog.
pag.* 36. 37.
&c.

I 3   with-

The State
of the con-
trouersie
with Card.
Bellarmine

without any further diftinction, or explication thereof. Wherupon fome learned men at home being different in opinions, the cafe was confulted abroad, where
all agreed (as before hath byn fhewed) that it could
not be taken wholy with fafety of confcience, and fo
alfo the Pope declared the cafe by two feuerall Breues.

I I. In the meane fpace it happened, that *M. Blackwell* being taken, was committed to prifon, and foone
after, as he had byn of opinion before, that the faid *Oath*
might be taken as it lay in a certayne fenfe; fo it being
offred vnto him, he tooke it himfelfe. Which thing
being noyfed abroad, and the fact generally mifliked
by all fortes of Catholicke people in other Realmes, as
offenfiue, and fcandalous in regard of his place, and perfon, fo much refpected by them : *Cardinall Bellarmine*, as
hauing had fome old acquaintance with him in former yeares, as it may feeme, refolued out of his particuler loue, & zeale to the Common caufe of Religion,
and fpeciall affection to his perfon, to write a letter
vnto him, therby to let him know what reportes, and
iudgment there was made of his fact, throughout thofe
partes of Chriftendome where he remayned, togeather
with his owne opinion alfo, which confifted in two
poynts, the one that the *Oath*, as it ftood, compounded of
different claufes, fome lawfull, & fome vnlawfull, could
not be taken with fafety of Confcience : the other, that
he being in the dignity he was of Prelacy, and Pa-
ftorall Charge, ought to ftand firme and conftant for
example of others, & rather to fuffer any kynd of danger
or domage, then to yield to any vnlawfull thing, fuch as
the Cardinall held this *Oath* to be.

I I I. This Letter was written vpon the 28. day of
September 1607. and it was fubfcribed thus in Latyn;

Admodum R.dᵉ Dom.ⁱˢ V.ᵉ

Frater & feruus in Chrifto.

Robertus Card. Bellarminus.

Which

Ca. Bellar.
his opinion
of taking
the Oath.

Which our Apologer translateth, *Your very Reuerēd Brother:* wheras the word *very Reuerend* in the letter, is gyuen to the Arch-priest, and not to *Card. Bellarmine,* which the interpreter knew well inough, but that wanting other matter, would take occasion of cauilling by a wilfull mistaking of his owne, as often he doth throughout this Answere to *Bellarmine,* as in part will appeare by the few notes which heere I am to set downe, leauing the more full Answere to the *Cardinall* himselfe, or some other by his appoyntment, which I doubt not, but will yield very ample satisfaction in that behalfe. For that, in truth, I fynd, that great aduantage is gyuen vnto him, for the defence of his said Epistle, and that the exceptions taken there against it, be very weake and light, and as easy to be dissolued by him, and his penne, as a thin mist by the beames of the sunne.

IIII. As for example, the first exception is (which no doubt were great, if it were true in such a man as *Cardinall Bellarmine* is) that he hath mistaken the whole State of the Questiō, in his writing to *M. Blackwell,* going about to impugne only the old *Oath* of *Supremacy,* in steed of this new *Oath,* entituled, *Of Allegiance:* but this is most cleerly refuted by the very first lynes almost of the letter it selfe. For that telling *M. Blackwell,* how sory he was vpon the report, that he had taken *illicitum Iuramentum,* an vnlasull *Oath,* he expoundeth presently, what *Oath* he meaneth, saying : *Not therfore (deare Brother) is that Oath lawsull, for that it is offered somwhat tempered & modifyed,* &c. Which is euidently meant of the new Oath of *Allegiance,* not only tempered with diuers lawfull clauses of Ciuill Obedience, as hath byn shewed, but interlaced also with other members, that reach to Religion: wheras the old *Oath* of *Supremacie,* hath no such mixture, but is playnly, and simply set downe, for absolute excluding the *Popes Supremacie* in causes Ecclesiasticall, and for making the King supreme Head of the Church in the same causes :

Pag. 44.

A Cauill.

Pag. 46.

Whether *Bellar.* mistaketh the state of the Question.

ᶜaufes: all which is moft euident by the Statutes made about the fame, from the 25 yeare of *King Henry* the 8. vnto the end of the raigne of *King Edward* the fixt.

The tytle of Supremacy.

V. Only I do heere note by the way, that the Apologer in fetting downe the forme of the *Oath* of *Supremacie* faith : *I A. B. do vtterly teftifie, and declare in my Confcience, that the Kings Highnes is the only Supreme Gouernour, as well in all caufes fpirituall as temporall,* wheras in the Statute of 26. of

Stat. 26. Henr 8.c.1.

K. *Henry* the 8. where the tytle of *Supremacy* is enacted, the wordes are thefe: *Be it enacted by this prefent Parlament, that the King our Soueraigne, his heires and fucceffors, fhalbe taken, accepted, and reputed the only Supreme Head in earth of the Church of England, called* Ecclefia Anglicana, *and fhall haue, & inioy, annexed, and vnited to the Imperiall Crowne of this Realme, as well the tytle and ftyle therof, as all honours, dig i yes, authori yes, annuityes, profitis, and commodi yes to the faid Dignity o Supreme Head of the faid Church, belonging &c.*

VI. And further, wheras two yeares after, an *Oath* was deuifed for confirmation heerof in Parlament, the

Stat. 28. H. 8.cap.10.

wordes of the *Oath* are fett downe: *That he fhall fweare to renounce vtterly, and relinquifh the Bifhop of* Rome, *and his Authority, power, and iurifdiction &c. And that from hence forth, he fhall accept, repute, and take the Kings M.*ᵗⁱᵉ *to be the only Supreme Head in earth of the Church of England &c. And that the refufers of this Oath, fhall be reputed traytors and fuffer the paynes of death &c.* And in other Statutes it is decreed, that it fhall be treafon to deny this title of headfhip to the King. And by like Decree of *Parlament*, it is declared vnder King *Edward*, what this Authority of headfhipp is, when

Stat. 1. Edo. 6.cap.2.

they fay: *For fo much as all Authority of Iurifdiction fpirituall, and temporall is deryued, & deduced from the Kings M.*ᵗⁱᵉ *as Supreme Head of thefe Churches, & Realmes of England and Ireland &c.*

VII. This was wont to be the doctryne of *Supremacy* in the tymes of *King Henry*, and *King Edward*, and it was death to deny this tytle, or not to fweare the fame: now

our

our Apologer thinketh it not good to giue it any longer to his Matie that now is, but calleth him only *Supreme Gouernour,* which is a new deuise taken from *Iohn Reynolds,* & other his fellowes, who aboue twenty yeares gone, being preſſed by his Aduerſary *M. Hart,* about calling *Q. Elizabeth, Head of the Church,* he denyeth flatly, that they called her ſo, but only *Supreme Gouerneſſe,* which I had thought they had done in regard of her ſex, that is not permitted to ſpeake in the Church. But now I perceaue they haue paſſed the ſame alſo ouer to his M.^{tie} not permitting him to inherite the tytles, eyther of *King Edward,* or *King Henry*; which miſliketh not vs at all, for that ſo farre they may paſſe heerin, as we may come to agree. For if they will vnderſtand by ſupreme Gouernour, the temporall Princes Supreme Authority ouer all perſons of his dominions, both Eccleſiaſticall, and Temporall, in temporall matters, excepting only Spirituall (wherin as yow haue heard a litle before *S. Ambroſe* told the Chriſtian Emperours of his tyme, that being Lay-men, they could not rightly meddle:) I ſee no great difficulty, which in this affayre would remayne betweene vs.

Conferéce in the Tower. cap. 1. diuiſ. 1. pa. 90.

VIII. To returne then to the Charge of ouerſight, and *groſſe miſtaking* (to vſe the Apologers words) layd by him to *Cardinal Bellarmine,* for impugning the ancienter *Oath of Supremacy,* inſteed of this later called, *Of Allegiance,* & *Of giuing the child a wrong name* (as he ſaith,) I ſee not by what leaſt colour, or ſhew of reaſon, it may ſtãd againſt him. For beſydes that which we haue ſaid before, of the *téperament,* & *modification* mentioned by him to be craftily couched in this later *Oath,* which by his letter he refuteth (I meane *of lawfull, and vnlawfull clauſes*) which muſt needes be vnderſtood of the ſecond Oath; he adioyneth preſently the côfutation of thoſe modifications, ſaying: *For yow know that thoſe kind of modifications, are nothing els, but ſleightes & ſubtilityes of Sathã, that the Catholicke faith, touching the*

Apolog. pag. 37.

K   Primacy

Primacy of the Sea Apostolicke, might eyther secretly , or openly be shott at . Lo heere he mentioneth both the *Oathes*, the one which shooteth *secretly* at the Primacy of the Sea Apostolicke (which is the later *Of Allegiance*) & the other that impugneth it *openly*, which is the first of the *Supremacy*. And as he nameth the secōd in the first place, so doth he principally prosecute the same, & proueth the vnlawfulnes therof, mentioning the other but only as by the way, for that it is as *Totū ad Partē* to the former, as a man can hardly speake of particuler mēbers of a body, without naming also the said body (as whē *S. Iames* inueigheth

Iac. 3. against the tōgue, he saith, *That it inflameth the whole body:*) so *Card.* all *Bellarmine* could hardly reproue the particuler branches of the Oath *Of Allegiance*, tending against sundry parts of the Popes *Primacie*, without mentioning the generall Oath of *Supremacy*, though it were not his purpose chiefly to impugne that, but the other. Which later *Oath*, albeit the Apologer sticketh not to say, that it toucheth not any part of the Popes Spirituall *Supremacy* : yet in the very next period, he contradicteth & ouerthroweth himselfe therin: For so much, as deuiding the said Oath

The Oath deuided into 14. partes. of *Allegiance* into 14. seuerall partes or parcels, twelue of them, at least, do touch the said *Supremacy* one way or other, as by examination yow will fynd, and we shall haue occasion after to declare more at large.

Apolog. pag. 49.   IX. As for example, he writeth thus : And that the Iniustice (saith he) as well as the error of *Bellarmine* his
,, grosse mistaking in this poynt, may yet be more cleerly
,, discouered ; I haue thought good to insert heere imme-
,, diatly the contrary conclusions to all the poynts and
,, Articles, wherof this other late *Oath* doth consist, wher-
,, by it may appeare, what vnreasonable and rebellious
,, poynts he would dryue his Ma.ties Subiects vnto, by
,, refusing the whole body of that *Oath*, as it is conceaued.
,, For he that shall refuse to take this *Oath*, must of necessity
,, hold these propositions following : *First that our Soue-*
raigne

raigne Lord King Iames *is not the lawfull King of this Kingdome,
and of all other his* Maties *Dominions. Secondly that the Pope by his
owne authority may depose,&c.* But who doth not see what
a simple fallacy this is, which the Logicians do call *A
composito ad diuisa* ,from denying of a compound, to inferre the denyall of all the parcels therin conteyned. As
if some would say, that *Plato* was a man borne in *Greece,*
of an excellent wit, skilfull in the Greeke language, most
excellent of all other Philosophers, and would require
this to be confirmed by an *Oath*, some *Platonist*, perhaps,
would be côtét to sweare it: but if some *Stoicke,* or *Peripa-
teticke,* or Professour of some other Sect in Philosophy,
should refuse the said *Oath,* in respect of the last clause,
might a man inferre against him in all the other clauses
also, *Ergò* he denyeth *Plato* to be a Man? He denyeth him
to be borne in *Greece,* he denyeth him to be of an excellét
wit, he denyeth him to be skilfull in the *Greeke* tongue,
&c. Were not this a bad kynd of arguing?

X. So in like manner, if an *Arrian,* or *Pelagian* Prince, ·Bad kinde
should exact an *Oath* at his Subiects hands, concerning of arguing.
diuers articles of Religion, that were belieued by them
both, and in the end, or middle therof, should insert
some clauses, sounding to the fauour of their owne
sect, for which the Subiect should refuse the whole body
of that *Oath,* as it was conceyued; cou'd the other in iustice accuse him, for denying all the seuerall articles of
his owne Religion also, which therin are mencyoned?
Who seeth not the iniustice of this manner of dealing?
And yet this is that which our Apologer vseth heere
with Catholicks, affirming in good earnest, that he
which refuseth the whole body of this *Oath,* as it is conceyued (in respect of some clauses therof that stand
against his Conscience, about matters of Religion) refuseth consequently euery poynt and parcell therof, and
must of necessity hold (in the first place) that our Soueraigne Lord King *Iames* is not the lawfull King of this

Kingdome, and of all other his Maties Dominions. The contrary wherof all Catholicks do both confeſſe, and profeſſe : & conſequently it is a meere calumniation that they deny this. But let vs ſee, how he goeth forward, in prouing this whole *Oath* to be lawfull to a Catholicke mans Conſcience.

Apol. pag. 52.

XI. And that the world (ſaith he) may yet further ſee, his Maties and whole States ſetting downe of this *Oath,* did not proceed from any new inuention of theirs, but as it is warranted by the word of God : So doth it take the example from an *Oath of Allegiance,* decreed a thouſand yeares agone, which a famous Councell then, togeather with diuers other Councels, were ſo farre from condemning (as the Pope now hath done this *Oath*) as I haue thought good to ſet downe their owne wordes heere in that purpoſe ; wherby it may appeare, that his Matie craueth nothing now of his Subiects in this *Oath,* which was not expreſly, and carefully commanded them by the Councels to be obeyed, without exception of perſons. Nay not in the very particuler poynt of *Equiuocation,* which his Matie in this *Oath* is ſo carefull to haue eſchewed : but yow ſhall heere ſee the ſaid Councels in their Decrees, as carefull to prouide for the eſchewing of the ſame ; ſo as, almoſt euery poynt of that Action, and this of ours, ſhall be found to haue relation, and agreeance one with the other, ſaue only in this ; that thoſe old Councels were carefull, and ſtraite in commanding the taking of the ſame; wheras by the contrary, he, that now vaunteth himſelfe to be Head of all Councells , is as carefull and ſtrait in the prohibition of all men, from the taking of this *Oath of Allegiance.* So he.

The Oath of Allegiance confirmed by the authoritie of Councels.

„
„
„
„
„
„
„
„

The difference betweene the ancient Councels, and the Popes Counſelling of the Catholiks.

XII. And I haue alledged his diſcourſe at large, to the end yow may better ſee his fraudulent manner of proceeding. He ſaith, That the example of this *Oath* is taken from an *Oath of Allegiance* decreed a thouſand
yeares

yeares agone in the Councels of *Toledo,* but especially
the fourth, which prouided also for the particuler poynt
of *Equiuocation*: But let any man read those Councels,
which are 13. in number, and if he fynd eyther any
forme of an *Oath* prescribed, or any mention of *Equiuocation,* but only of flat lying and perfidious dealing; let
him discredit all the rest that I do write. And if he
fynd none at all, as most certainly he shall not; then let
him consider of the bad cause of this Apologer, that
dryueth him to such manner of dealing, as to auouch,
*Euery point of that Action to haue agreeance with the offering of
this Oath.*

XIII. True it is that those Councels of *Toledo,*
vpon certayne occasions, which presently we shall declare, do recommend much to the subiects of *Spayne,* both
Gothes and *Spaniards;* that they do obserue their *Oath* of
fidelity made vnto their Kings, especially vnto *Sisenandus,*
for whose cause principally this matter was first treated
in the fourth Councel of *Toledo,* but no speciall forme is
prescribed by the said Councell: nor is *Equiuocation* so
much as named therin, but only (as hath bene said)
Iurare mendaciter, to sweare falsely, as the wordes of the
Councel are. Which how far it is from the true nature
of Equiuocation hath bene lately and largly demonstrated as yow know.

XIV. The cause of the treatie of this matter in the
4. Councell of *Toledo,* was, for that one *Sisenandus* a
Nobleman of the bloud of the *Gothes* and a great Captaine, taking opportunitie of the euill life of his
King *Suintila,* whome he had serued, did by some violence (as most of the * Spanish Historiographers write,
though confirmed afterward by the Common-wealth,
and proued a very good King) and, as *Paulus Aemilius* in
his French Historie recordeth, by helpe of *Dagobert*
King of *France,* put out the said *Suintila*: and fearing lest
the same people that had made defection to him, might

K 3   by

*Conc. Tole.
4.can. 74.*

The occasion of gathering
the 4. Councell of Toledo.

* See Rode.
Tolet.lib.2.
dereb. Hist.
c.19. Sätius
par. 2. hist.
Hisp.c.27.
Ioan. Vaseus in
Chron.Hist.
num.631.

by the same meanes fall from him againe, he procured in the third yeare of his raigne, this fourth Councell of *Toledo*, to be celebrated of 70. Prelates, as some say, and as others, of 68. hoping by their meanes, that his safety in the Crowne should be confirmed. Wherupon it is set downe, in the Preface of the said Councell, that comming into the same, accompanyed with many noble and honorable persons of his trayne; *Coram sacerdotibus Dei humi prostratus, cum lachrymis, & gemitibus pro se interueniedum postulauit:* He prostrate on the ground before the Priests of God, with teares and sobbes, besought them to make intercession vnto God for him. And after that, religiously *exhorted the Synod to be myndfull of the Fathers Decrees, for confirmation of Ecclesiasticall rytes &c.* Wherupon after seauenty and three Decrees made, about Ecclesiasticall matters, which whosoeuer will read, shall fynd them wholy against the *Protestants*, as setting downe, & describing the whole vse of the Catholicke Church then in *Spayne* (which concurred with our first Primitiue Church of *England* conforme to that which now also is scene there) they in the last Canon, which was the 74. turned themselues to treat in like manner of matters of the Common wealth, appoynting the order how their Kings for the tyme to come, should be established: *Defuncto in pace Principe, Primates Gen: is cum Sacerdotibus, successorem Regni, consilio communi, constituant.* The Prince being dead in peace, let the Nobility of the Nation, togeather with the Priests, by common counsell, appoynt a successour in the kingdome &c.

     XV. And then next to this, they do excommunicate all those, that shall attempt the destruction of the present King, or shall breake their *Oath* of Fidelity made vnto him: *Aut si quis præsumptione Tyrannica Regni fastigium vsurpauerit:* or if any shall, by Tyrannical presumption, vsurpe the dignity of the Crowne, *aut Sacramentum fidei sua, quod pro Patriæ, Gentisque Gothorum statu, vel conseruatione*

Regiæ

Conc. Tole.
4. in Præ-
fat.

Anno Domini 633.

The care
of the
Councell
for Ciuill
Fidelity to
be obser-
ued to the
King.

Regiæ falutis pollicitus eſt , violauerit, aut Regem neci attrectauerit: If any man ſhall violate the Oath or his fidelitie, which he hath promiſed for the ſtate , or conſeruation of his Countrey, and Gothiſh Nation, and of the Kings ſafety, or ſhall attempt the Kings death &c. *Lett him be accurſed* (ſay they) *in the ſight of God the Father, and of his Angels , and caſt out from the Catholicke Church , which by his periury he hath profaned; and let him be ſeparated from all Society of Chriſtians, togeather with all his aſſociates in ſuch atteptes.* And this curſe they do renew and repeat diuers tymes in that Canon; *Vt hæc tremenda, & toties iterata ſententia , nullum ex nobis præ-ſenti atque æterno condemnet iudicio ;* that this dreadfull and often iterated ſentence of excommunication , do not condemne any of vs with iudgement preſent , and euerlaſting alſo , if we incurre the ſame.

XVI. This then was the great care which thoſe ancient Fathers (wherof the holy and learned man *S. Iſidorus,* Archbiſhop of *Siuill* was the firſt that ſubſcribed) had of the dutifull obedience , & fidelity of ſubiects to-wards their Princes, vnto whome they had once ſworne the ſame. But as for any particuler forme of *Oath* there preſcribed, wherby this new *Oath* now required *Of Alle-giāce* may be framed, that hath ſo many clauſes therin of ſcruple of cōſcience to the receauer , I fynd none at all. And no doubt , but if this King *Siſenandus* ſhould haue exacted of any of theſe Biſhops , or other his ſubiects, ſuch an Oath of Allegiance, as ſhould haue beene mixed with any clauſes preiudiciall to any of thoſe points of Eccleſiaſticall affaires , which are handled and decreed by them, in the ſaid 73. precedent Canons of this Coū-cell, or others contrary to their Conſcience or iudg-ment in Religion : they would haue beene ſo farre of from yielding therunto, as they would rather haue gi-uen their liues, then their conſents to ſuch an Oath .

XVII. But to go forward, and ſpeake a word or two more of this Councell of *Toledo.* After thoſe 70. Fathers

Can. 74.

No forme of Oath preſcribed by the Councell.

Fathers had taken this order for the temporall fafetie of their Prince, and *Gothish* Nation (for that was a principall point that none fhould be admitted to the Crowne, but of that race) they turne their fpeach to the prefent King *Sifenandus,* and to his fucceffours, making this exhortation vnto him. *Te quoque præfentem Regem, ac futuros ætatum fequentium Principes, humilitate, qua debemus, depofcimus, vt moderati & mites erga fubiectos exiftentes &c.* We with due humility, do require at your hâds alfo that are our prefent King, and at the hands of thofe that fhall enfue in future tymes, that yow be moderate and myld towards your fubiects, and do rule your people committed vnto yow by God, in iuftice and piety; and do yield to Chrift, the giuer of all your power, good correfpondence by raigning ouer them, in humility of harte, and indeauour of good workes &c. And we do promulgate here againft all Kings to come this fentence; *Vt fi quis ex eis, contra reuerentiam legum, fuperba dominatione, & faftu Regio in flagitijs crudeliffimam poteftatem in populis exercuerit, Anathematis fententia à Chrifto Domino condemnetur. &c.* That if any of them fhall againft the reuerence of the lawes, by proud domination, and Kingly haughtines, exercife wickednes, and cruell power vpon the people committed to their charge, let him be condemned of Chrift, by the fentence of curfe; and let him haue his feparation, and iudgment from God himfelfe.

XVIII. After this, for better eftablifhment of the faid prefent King *Sifenandus,* they do confirme the depofition and expulfion, from the Crowne, of the forefaid King *Suintila,* (which by error of the print, is called in the Booke of Councells, *Semithilana*) pronouncing both him, his wife, and their brother, to be iuftly expulfed for their wickednes: though the forefaid *S. Ifidorus,* then liuing, and writing the Hiftory of *Spayne,* dedicated to this King *Sifenandus,* doth fpeake much good of the * former parte of the other King his life and raigne.

And

What the Councell demaûded at K. Sifenandus his handes towards his people.

The depofition of K. Suintila confirmed by the Councell.
⁴ Se Chro. Vafæi nu. 631.

And fynally some fyue yeares after this agayne in the sixt Councell of *Toledo*, being gathered togeather in the same Church of *S. Leocadia*, the said Bishops, togeather with the Nobility, did make this law, and prescribed this forme of *Oath* to all Kings of that nation, *Vt quisquis succedentium, temporum Regni sortitus fuerit apicem, non anteà conscendat Regiam Sedem, quàm inter reliquas condiciones, Sacramento pollicitus fuerit, hanc se Catholicam non permissurum eos violare fidem.* That whatsoeuer future King, shall obtayne the height of this Kingdome, he shall not be permitted to ascend to the Royall seate therof, vntill he haue sworne, among other conditions, that, he will neuer suffer his subiects to violate this Catholicke faith. Marke that he saith (*this*) which was the Catholicke faith then held in *Spayne*, and explicated in those Councels of *Toledo*; the particulers wherof do easely shew, that they were as opposite to the Protestant faith, as we are now.

Conc. Tol. 6. ca. 3.

An Oath prescribed by the Councell to Kings.

XIX. So as, all this is against the Apologer: for that in these Councells no particuler forme of any Oath was set downe, or exhibited at all to Subiects, that we can read of, but only in generall, it is commanded, That all do keepe their *Oath* of *Allegiance* sworne to their Princes, at their first entrance, or afterward. Which thing, no Pope did euer forbid, and all English Catholicks at this day do offer willingly to performe the same to this Matie; and consequently, all that ostentation made by the Minister before, *That this Oath is no new inuention: That it doth take the example from an Oath of Allegiance decreed a thousand yeares gone, by a famous Councell: That the Councel prouided in particuler for the poynts of Equiuocation: That almost euery poynt of that action hath agreeance with this of ours, sauing only in this, that the Councell was carefull, & straite in commanding the taking of the same, and Pope* Paulus *carefull and strayt in the prohibition &c.*

L   XX.

XX. All this, I fay, falleth by it felfe to the ground: for fo much, as neyther that Councell commanded the taking of any *Oath*, nor prefcribed any forme to Subiects, nor Pope *Paulus* prohibiteth this, fo farre as it concerneth Temporall, and Ciuill Obedience, as hath byn declared. And whatfoeuer the Apologer cyteth more out of thefe Councels, the meaneft Reader, by looking vpon it, will eafely efpy, that it maketh nothing at all for him, or againft vs, and confequently the entring into the narration of this matter, with fo great oftentation, as, *That the world may fee, that it proceeded not of any new inuention, but is warranted by the word of God, authorized by fo auncient a Councell,* and the like: All this (I fay) was needlcs; for fo much, as nothing is found in this Councell that agreeth with our cafe, but only the naming and recommending of an Oath or fidelity, wherin we alfo fully agree and confent with our Aduerfary.

The fecond Part of this Paragraph.

O w then to come to the particuler Anfwere of our Apologer to the Card.lls Letter, he doth for diuers leaues togeather, as it were, dally with him, picking quarrells here and there, vntill he come to the mayne charge of contradiction of himfelf, to himfelf, not only in this Letter, but throughout all his workes. And albeit I doubt not, but that the Card.ll or fome other by his appointment, will difcuffe all thefe matters largly and

fuffisufficiently: yet for so much, as I haue promised to giue you my iudgment of all, I shall briefly in like máner lay forth what I haue obserued about these pointes.

XXII. Page 57. of his Apology he writeth thus: *That some of such Priests, and Iesuits, as were the greatest traytors, and fomentors of the greatest conspiracyes, against her late Maiesty, gaue vp F. Robert Bellarmyne, for one of their greatest authorities, and Oracles.* And for proofe he citeth in the margent *Campian* and *Hart: See the Conference in the Tower.* By which I discouer a greater abuse then I could haue imagined, would euer haue come from a man carefull of his credit: for I haue seene and perused the *Conference* of M.r D. *Iohn Reynolds* with M. *Iohn Hart* in the Tower, vpon the yeare 1583. two yeares after the death of F. *Campian,* and there it appeareth indeed that the said M. *Hart* alleadgeth diuers tymes the opinions and proofes of F. *Robert Bellarmyne,* then publick Reader of Controuersies in *Rome,* but alwayes about matters of Deuinity and Controuersies, and neuer about Treasons or Conspiracyes. And as for F. *Campian,* he is neuer read to mention him, eyther in the one or the other. Consider then the deceitfull equiuocation here vsed, that for so much, as M. *Hart* alleadged F. *Robert Bellarmine* sometymes in matters of Controuersie in that conference, therefore both *he* & F. *Campian* alleadged him for *an Author and Oracle of Conspiracy* against the Queene. And how can these things be defended with any shew or probability of truth?

XXIII. Page 60. he frameth a great reprehension against the Card.ll for that in his letter he saith, that this *Oath* is not therfore lawfull, *for that it is offered as tempered and modified.* Whereupon the Apologer playeth, and insulteth, as though the Card.ll had reprehended the téperate speech therin vsed, adding, That in *Luther* and others of the Protestant writers, we mislike their bold & free speaking, as comming from the diuells instinct.

L 2 And

Card. Bellar. wrógfully charged with conspiracyes.

,, And now if we fpeake (faith he) moderately, and tem-
,, perately, it muft be tearmed the diuells craft, and ther-
,, fore we may iuftly complaine with Chrift, That when
,, we mourne, they will not lament, and when we pype
,, they will not dance. And neyther *Iohn Baptift* his feuerity,
,, nor Chrift his meeknes can pleafe them, who buyld but
,, to their owne Monarchy, vpon the ground of their
,, owne Traditions, and not to Chrift, &c. Thus he, and
much more exprobration to this effect, that we miflike
the temperate ftyle and fpeach vfed in this *Oath* of
Allegiance. But all is quite miftaken, and the Apologer
hath iuft caufe to blufh at this error, if it were error
and not wilfull miftaking. For that *Bellarmyne* doth not
fay, that this *Oath* is temperate in wordes, but tempered in matter, *aliquo modo temperatum & modificatum*:
in a certayne fort *tempered* and *modified* by the offerers, in
fetting downe fome claufes lawfull, touching Cyuill
Obedience, and adioyning others vnlawfull, that concerne Confcience, and Religion. Which meaning of
Bellarmyne is euident by the example, which he alleadgeth, of the Enfignes of the Emperour *Iulian*, out of *S.
Gregory Nazianzen*, to wit; That the images of Pagan
Gods were mingled, and combined togeather with the
Emperours picture, & therby fo *tempered*, and *modified*,
as a man could not adore the one, without the other.
Which being fo, let the indifferent Reader confider
what abufe is offered to Card.all *Bellarmyne*, in charging him to miflike temperate fpeach in the forme of
this *Oath*, which of likelyhood he neuer thought on, and
yet theron to found fo great an inference, as to accufe
him to buyld therby to a *Monarchy, and not to Chrift*. Is this
a token of want of better matter, or no?

    XXIV. Page 62. the Apologer hauing faid with
,, great vehemency of affeueration, That heauen and
,, earth are no further afunder, then the profeffion of a
,, Temporall Obedience, to a Temporall King, is diffe-
,, rent

A volun-
tary mifta-
king of te-
perate for
tempered.

rent from any thing belonging to the Catholicke faith , or Supremacy of *S. Peter* (which we graunt also, if it be meere Temporall Obedience without mixture of other clauses:) he proposeth presently two questions for application of this to his purpose. First this: *As for the Catholicke Religion* (saith he) *can there be one word found in all this Oath, tending to matter of Religion?* The second thus: *Doth he that taketh it, promise to beleeue, or not to beleeue any article of Religion?* Wherunto I answere first to the first, and then to the second. To the first, that if it be graunted, that power, and authority of the Pope, and Sea Apostolicke left by Christ, for gouerning his Church in all occasions & necessityes , be any point belonging to Religion among Catholicks, thē is there not only some one word, but many sentences, yea ten or twelue articles, or branches therin, *tending* and *sounding* that way as before hath bene shewed.

XXV. To the second question may make answere euery clause in effect of the Oath it self. As for example the very first: *I A.B. doe truly, and sincerely acknowledge , professe, testify, & declare in my Conscience, that the Pope neither of himself, nor by any authority of the Sea or Church of Rome, hath any power & authority to &c.* doth not this include eyther beliefe, or vnbeliefe? Againe: *I doe further sweare, that I doe frō my hart abhorre, detest, & abiure: as impious, & hereticall, that damnable doctrine, & position, That Princes which be excommunicated, and depriued by the Pope , may bo deposed &c.* Doth not heere the swearer promise, not to beleeue that doctrine which he so much detesteth? How thē doth the Apologer so grosly forget, and contradict himself, euen then, when he goeth about to proue contradictions in his Aduersary ?

XXVI. It followeth consequently in the Oath : *And I doe beleeue , and in Conscience am resolued, That neyther the Pope, nor any person whatsoeuer , hath power to absolue me from this Oath, or any part therof.* These wordes are plaine as yow see. And what will the Apologer say heere ? Is nothing

,,
,,
,,
Two questions proposed and solued.

1.

2.

Clauses of beliefe or not beliefe in the Oath.

Pag. 12.

promised

promifed in thofe wordes to be belieued, or not to be belieued?

XXVII. But now we come to the contradictions of Cardinall *Bellarmyne*, wherof the Apologer taketh occafion to treate, for that the Cardinall affirmeth in one part of his letter, That neyther his Maiefty of *England*, nor any Prince elfe, hath caufe to feare violence from the Pope; for that it was neuer heard of, from the Churches infancy, vntill this day, that any Pope did commaund, That any Prince, though an Hereticke, though an Ethnicke, though a Perfecutour, fhould be murthered, or did allow the murther, when it was done by an other. Which affertion, the Apologer to improue, bringeth in examples firft of doctrine, that *Bellarmyne* himfelf doth hold, That Princes vpon iuft caufes may be depofed by Popes: and then of facts, That diuers Emperours haue bene depofed, and great warres raifed againft them, by Popes, as *Bellarmyne* in his workes doth confeffe, and cannot deny, and confequently doth contradict himfelf. But furely this feemeth to me a very fimple oppofition or contradiction. For who doth not fee, that thefe things may well ftand togeather, are not oppofite, and may be both true; That Popes vpon iuft caufes, haue waged warres againft diuers Princes, and Potentates; and yet neuer caufed any to be vnlawfully made away, murthered, or allowed of their murthers committed by others. For, may not we fay iuftly, that warlike Princes are no murtherers, though in the Acts of warres thefelues, many haue bene flaine, by their authority and commandement? Or may not we deliuer our Iudges of *England*, from the cryme of murther, though many mens deathes haue proceeded from them, by way of Iuftice? No man (I thinke) will deny it.

XXVIII. And fo if fome Popes haue had iuft warres with fome Princes, Kinges or Emperours, or haue per-
fuaded

Apolog. 38. & 64.

Bell. lib. 5. de Pon. c. 8. & lib. 3. cap. 16.
"
"
"
"

ſuaded themſelues, that they were iuſt, in reſpect of
ſome ſuppoſed diſorders of the ſaid Princes (as here is
mentioned the warre, and other hoſtile proceedings
of Pope Gregory the ſeauenth againſt the Emperour
Henry the fourth) this is not contrary to the ſaying of
*Cardinall Bellarmyne, That no Pope euer commaunded any Prince to
be murthered, or allowed therof, after it was done by an other.*
For as for that which heere is affirmed by the Apologer, *That the Pope was inraged at the Emperour* Henry
the 5. *for giuing buriall to his Fathers dead corps, after the
Pope had ſtirred him vp againſt his Father, and procured his ruyne,*
neyther proueth the matter, nor is altogeather true,
as heere it is alleadged. Not the firſt: for this proueth not, that the Pope eyther commaunded or
procured this death, which *Bellarmyne* denyed. Not the
ſecond: for that the two Authours by him cyted in his
margent, to wit, *Platina* and *Cuſpinian,* doe not auerre the
ſame. For in *Platina* I finde no ſuch thing at all; and
Cuſpinian his wordes are plaine to the contrary: That
when *Henry* the Father was dead, and buried in a Mo-
naſtery at *Liege,* his Sonne would not make peace with
the Biſhop of that place, called * *Otbert,* except the
dead body were pulled out of the graue againe, as
it was, and ſo remayned for ſiue yeares.

XXIX. And againe *Cuſpinian* writeth, That the
report was, that *Gregory* the 7. did before his death ab-
ſolue the Emperour; but that his Sonne *Henry* the 5.
and his followers neuer left to ſollicite the ſucceeding
Popes vntill he was excommunicated againe, & thereupon
had afterward this Chriſtian buriall denyed him. And
how then, is all this aſcribed to the Pope, which proceeded from the Sonne againſt his Father? Our Apologer ſaith, That he was ſett on by the Pope to rebell
againſt him, but this his witneſſes affirme not. For
Cuſpinian ſaith that it was, *Suaſu Marchionis Theobaldi, Be-
rengary* Comitis Noricorum, *& Ottonis ſibi ex materna ſtirpe
cognati*

*Touching
Henry the
4.*

Pag. 65. 66.
*Platin. &
Cuſp. in vi-
ta Henrici
4.*

*Cuſp. in
Henrico
quarto.*

* *See Nau-
cler. part. 2.
gen.* 37. *in
anno* 1106.
*& Crantz.
lib.* 5. *Saxo.
cap.* 24.

*Cuſpin. in
Henrico 4.*

cognati. And in this commonly agree all other Authors, as ᵃ *Vrspergensis*, who then liued , ᵇ *Crantzius*, ᶜ *Sigonius*, ᵈ *Nauclerus*, and others. And why then is this so vniustly layed vpon the Pope? What Author can he bring for it, that auoucheth the same ? Why is it couertly cast in, as though this matter apperteyned to *Gregory* the seauenth, who in his life had warres with *Henry* the fourth, but yet dyed before him? Heere then nothing is so apparent, as the desire to say much against Popes, with neuer so litle occasion, and lesse proofe. But let vs go forward.

XXX. In the second place he produceth the approbation of the slaughter of the late *King* of *France* by Pope *Sixtus* in his speech in the Consistory: But no record of credit, eyther in *Rome* or elswhere, can be found to testify, that any such speech euer was had by Pope *Sixtus*. And I vnderstand that diuers Cardinalls are yet liuing, who were then present in the first Consistory, after that newes arriued, who deny that *Sixtus* euer vttered any such words, as of the allowance of that horrible fact, though he might, and did highly admire the strange prouidence of God, in chastising by so vnexpected a way, so foule and impious a murther, as that King had committed vpon a Prince, Bishop, and Cardinall (and those neerest of bloud vnto his Maiesty of *England*) without any forme of iudgment at all. And that a spectacle heerby of Gods Iustice was proposed vnto Princes, to be moderate in their power, and passions : for that in the midst of his great and Royall army, and corporall guardes, he was strangely slaine by a simple vnarmed man, when nothing was lesse expected, or feared. Nor can any thing be more improbable or ridiculous to be imagined, then that which is heere affirmed by our Apologer (and yet, he saith, *he is sure therof*) *That this friar, which killed the King, should haue bene canonized for the fact, if some Cardinalls, out of their wisedome,*

had

had not reſiſted the ſame. No ſuch thing being euer ſo much as imagined, or conſulted of, as many doe teſtify who were then in *Rome.* So as nothing is more common here, then bold aſſertions without wittneſſes.

XXXI. And the like may be ſaid to his third example of the late Queene of *England,* againſt whoſe life (he ſaith) that ſo many practiſes, and attempts were made, *and directly inioyned to thoſe traytors, by their Conſeſſours, and plainly authorized by the Popes allowance.* So he ſaith. But if a man would aske him, how he can proue, that thoſe things were ſo *directly inioyned, and plainly authorized,* what anſwere will he make? Yow ſhall heare it in his owne wordes, for he hath but one : *For verification* (ſaith he) *there needeth no more proofe, then that neuer Pope, eyther then or ſince, called any Church-man in queſtion, for medling in thoſe treaſonable conſpiracyes.* And needeth no more (Syr) but this, to condemne both Conſeſſours and Popes of conſpiring the laſt Queenes death, *That no Pope hath called in queſtion, or puniſhed any Cleargy-man for ſuch like attempts?* Wnat if he neuer knew of any ſuch attempt? What if he neuer heard of any Clergy-man to be accuſed therof, except ſuch as were put to death by the Queene her ſelf, either culpable or not culpable? What if he ſaw ſome ſuch ridiculous falſe deuiſes, made againſt ſome Prieſts to make their whole company and cauſe odious, as iuſtly diſcredited with him all their other clamours and calumnious accuſations in that behalfe? As that of *Squier,* induced (as was ſayed) by *Fa. VValpole* in *Spaine* to poyſon the Queenes chayre, or the Earle of *Eſſex* his ſaddle, which was ſo monſtrous a fiction, and ſo plainly proued for ſuch in forrayne Countryes (and ſo conſeſſed by the miſerable feliow at his death) as tooke all credit from like deuiſes in theſe attemptes, of holding the Queene in perpetuall frightes, to the end, ſhe ſhou'd neuer attend to the true way of remedy.

XXXII. And with what little care of ſincerity,

Apolog. pag. 67.

Prieſtes put to death for fayned cōſpiracies.

An. 1598.

M   or

or of punctuall truth, all theſe things are here, and
elſwhere, caſt out at randome, to make a ſound and
noiſe in the Readers eares, appeareth ſufficiently in the
very next ſequent wordes, wherein ſpeaking of Doctor *Sanders* he ſaieth : *That whoſoeuer will looke vpon his
Bookes, will fynde them filled with no other Doctrine then this.* And
will any man thinke it probable or poſſible that ſo
many bookes as Doctor *Sanders* hath written, both in
Latyn and Engliſh, and of ſo different arguments concerning Religion, haue no other Doctrine in them, but
this of killing, and murthering of Princes? And that
other aſſertion alſo, that enſueth within very few lines
after, againſt Cardinall *Bellarmynes* whole Workes,
*That all his large and great Volumes are filled with contradi-
ctions,* wherof we are to treat more preſently. Now
only I doe note the facility, and cuſtome of ouerlaſhing
in this Apologer.

XXXIII. To conclude then about Queene *Elizabeth.* Albeit *Pius Quintus,* and ſome other Popes did
excommunicate her, and cut her of from the body of
the Catholicke Church by Eccleſiaſticall Cenſures, in
regard of her perſecuting Catholicke Religion: yet did
I neuer know it hitherto proued, that any Pope procured or conſented to any priuate violence againſt her
perſon : albeit, if the forealledged Statute of the 28.
yeare of King *Henry* the 8. be true, wherin it is determined both by the King himſelf, his Counſell, and
whole Parlament, as by the Archbiſhop *Cranmer,* with
his Doctors, in his Iudiciall Seat of the Arches, that
Lady *Elizabeth* was not legitimate, nor that her mother
was euer King *Henryes* true wife (which once being
true, could neuer afterward by any humane power
be made vntrue, or amended to the preiudice of a
third, rightly by due ſucceſſion intereſſed therin:) &

if, as the whole Parlament teſtifyed, it ſhould be
Againſt all honour, equity, reaſon, and good conſcience, that the
ſaid

said I.a. *Elizabeth, should at any tyme possesse the said Crowne,* then the said Popes, respecting in their said sentence (as it is certayne they did) the actuall right of the Queene of *France* and *Scotland*, and of her noble issue his Matie that now is, they might proceed, as they did, against the other, for her removall (whome they held for an vsurper) in fauour of the true inheritours oppressed by her, not only by spirituall, but temporall armes also, as against a publicke Malefactor and intruder contrary to right and conscience. And I cannot see, how this fawning Apologer, can eyther without open vntruth, or manifest iniury to his Maiesty, auerre the contrary. Which being true, doth greatly iustify the endeauours and desires of all good Catholicke people, both at home and abroad against her, their principall meaning being euer knowne to haue bene the deliuerance, & preferment of the true Heire, most wrongfully kept out, & iniustly persecuted for righteousnes sake.

XXXIIII. This then being so, and nothing proued at all against Popes for their murthering attempts against Princes, which *Cardinall Bellarmyne* denyed : yet this Apologer, as if he had proued much against him, in this point of contradicting himself, he writeth thus : *But who can wonder at this contradiction of himself in this point, when his owne great Volumes are so filled with contradictions, which when either he, or any other shall euer be able to reconcile, I will then belieue that he may easily reconcile this impudent strong denyall of his, in his letter, of any Popes medling against Kings.* Wherin is to be noted first, that wheras Card.^{ll} *Bellarmine* doth deny any Popes murthering of Princes, this man calleth it, *An impudent strong deniall of any Popes medling against Kings,* as though medling, and murthering were all one. Is not this good dealing? Truely if the Card.^{ll} had denyed, that euer any Pope had dealt, or medled against any King, or Prince, vpon any occasion whatsoeuer, it had beene a *strong denyall* indeed : but for so much, as

he

Q. Elizab. against cõscience held the Crown from his Maiestyes Mother 44. yeares.

Vniust dealing against the Cardinall.

he faith no fuch thing, I maruaile of the Apologers proceeding in this behalfe, for with the word *impudent* I will not meddle. But let vs heare him yet further.

XXXV. *And that I may not feeme* (faith he) *to imitate him, in affirming boldly that, which I no waies can proue, I will therefore fend the Reader, to looke for wittneffes of his contradictions in fuch places here mentioned in his owne booke.* Thus he, very confidently, as you fee, And verily I cannot but maruaile, that he knowing how many men of learning would looke vpon the places themfelues, (for I vnderftand now alfo that the book is out in latyn) would not be afhamed in him felf, to fuffer their iudgement of him and his doings in this behalfe: albeit he had not refpected the Cardinals anfwere, which muft nedes be with exceeding aduantage againft him, fuch as, in truth, I am afhamed for Countrey fake, that ftrangers fhould laugh vs to fcorne for fuch manner of writing. For if I doe vnderftand any thing, and that myne owne eyes, and iudgement doe not deceaue me, this Apologer will remayne vnder, in all & euery one of thefe oppofitions, no one of them being defenfible in the nature of a true

contradiction, and confequently *Cardinall Bellarmynes* great volumes of Controuerfies, will not only, not be proued *full of Contradictions* by this taft here giuen, as is pretended: but will rather be infinitly iuftifyed; that in fo many great Volumes, this Author hath not bene able to picke out any better contradictions then thefe. Wherof againe, I muft fay and auouch, that no one feemeth to me any contradiction at all, if they be well examined.

XXXVI. And though I meane not to difcuffe them all in this place, nor the greater part of them, they being eleuen in number, as hath bene faid, both for breuityes fake, and not to peruent the Cardinalls owne Anfwere, and fatisfaction therin (which I doubt not but

but will be very fufficient, and learned:) yet three or
foure I fhall touch only, for examples fake, thereby to
giue the Reader matter to make coniecture of the reſt.
This then he beginneth his liſt of eleuen contradictions
againſt the ſaid Cardinall.

XXXVII. Firſt in his bookes of Iuſtification (ſaith
he) *Bellarmyne* affirmeth, that for the vncertainty of our
owne proper righteouſnes, and for auoyding of vayne
glory, it is moſt ſure and ſafe, to repoſe our whole confidence in the alone mercy and goodnes of God: which
propoſition of his, is directly contrary to the diſcourſe,
& current of all his fiue bookes *De Iuſtificatione*, wherin
the ſame is conteyned &c. Of this firſt contradiction
we haue ſaid ſomewhat before, to wit, That it is
ſtrange, that fiue whole bookes ſhould be brought in, as
contradictory to one propoſition. For how ſhall the
Reader try the truth of this obiection? Shall he be
bound to read all *Bellarmynes* fiue bookes, to ſee whether it
be true or no? Had it not bene more plaine dealing
to haue alleadged ſome one ſentence, or concluſion
contradictory to the other? But now ſhall we ſhew,
that there can be no ſuch contradiction betwixt the
ſentence of one part of his ſaid Booke of *Iuſtification*, &
the whole diſcourſe or current of the reſt: for that
Bellarmyne doth make all the matter cleere, by ſoyling
three ſeuerall Queſtions in one Chapter, which is the
ſeauenth of the fifth Booke here cyted.

XXXVIII. The three Queſtions are theſe, about
Fiducia, quæ in meritis collocari poſsit, what hope and confidence, may be placed, by a Chriſtian man, in his
good workes, and merites. The firſt Queſtion is,
whether good workes, in a Chriſtian man, doe in-
creaſe hope and confidence by their own nature, and
the promiſe of reward made vnto them? And *Bellarmyne* anſwereth that they doe: and proueth it by many
places of Scriptures, as that of *Toby* the 4. where it

The firſt
ſuppoſed
contradi-
ction.
*Bellar. de
luſtific. lib.
5.cap.7.
Apol.68.*

Three
Queſtions
about Cō-
fidence in
merits anſ-
wered by
Bellarmi-
ne.
I.

is

Tob. 4.

Iob. 11.

1.Tim.3.

is faied : That *almes-deeds fhall giue great confidence, and hope to the doers therof in the fight of God.* And *Iob* fayeth : *That he which liueth iuftly, fhall haue great confidence, and hope, and fhall fleep fecurely.* And S. Paul to *Timothy* faith : *That who-foeuer fhall minifter well, fhall haue great confidence, &c.* And I omit diuers other plaine places of Scriptures, and Fathers there alleadged by him, which the Reader may there perufe to his comfort, fhewing euidently, that the confcience of a vertuous life, and good workes, doth giue great confidence to a Chriftian man, both while he liueth, and efpecially when he commeth to dye.

2.

XXXIX. The fecond Queftion is, whether this being fo, a man may place any confidence wittingly in his owne merits, or vertuous life. And it is anfwered, That he may ; fo it be with due circumftances of humility, for auoyding pride, and prefumption. For that a man feeling the effect of Gods grace in himfelf, wherby he hath bene directed to liue well, may alfo hope, that God will crowne his gifts in him, as S. *Augu-ftines* wordes are. And many examples of Scriptures are alleadged there by Card.ll *Bellarmyne* of fundry holy Saints, Prophets and Apoftles, that vpon iuft occafion mentioned their owne merits, as gifts from God that gaue them hope and confidence of his mercifull reward : and namely that faying of S. *Paul : I haue fought a good fight, I haue confummated my courfe, I haue kept my faith &c.* and then addeth, that in regard hereof, *Repofita eft mihi Corona Iuftitiæ,* A crowne of Iuftice is laid vp for me, which God the iuft Iudge fhall reftore vnto me.

2.Tim.4.

3.

XL. The third Queftion is (fuppofing the forefaid determinations) what counfaile were to be giuen : Whether it be good to put confidence in a mans owne merits or no ? whereunto Card.ll *Bellarmyne* anfwereth, in the words fet downe by the Apologer, *That for the vncer-tainty of our owne proper Iuftice, and for auoyding the perill of vaine*

vaine glory, the surest way is to repose all our confidence in the only mercy and benignity of God; from whome and from whose grace our merits proceed. So as albeit Card.[ll] *Bellarmyne* doth confesse, that good life, and vertuous acts doe giue hope, and confidence of themselues, and that it is lawfull also by the example of auncient Saints, for good men to comfort themselues with that hope and confidence: yet the surest way is to repose all in the benignity and mercy of almighty God, who giueth all, and is the Authour, as well of the grace, as of the merits, and fruites of good workes that ensue therof. And thus hath Cardinall *Bellarmyne* fully explicated his mynd in this one Chapter, about *Confidence in good workes,* by soluing the foresaid three different Questions, wherof the one is not contrary to the other, but may all three stand togeather. And how then is it likely, that the foresaid proposition, *of reposing our Confidence in the mercy of God,* should be *contradictory,* as this man saith, *to the whole discourse and current of all his fiue Bookes of Iustification?* Let one only sentence be brought forth, out of all these fiue Bookes that is truly contradictory, and I shall say he hath reason in all the rest of his ouerlashing.

XLI. His second obiected contradiction is as good as this, which he setteth downe in these wordes. [a] *God* (saieth Bellarmine) *doth not incline a man to euill, eyther naturally or morally :* and presently after he affirmeth the contrary, saying: [b] *That God doth not incline to euill naturally but morally.* But this is a plaine fallacy of the Apologer, for that the word *morally* is taken heere in two different senses, which himself could not but see. For first Card.[ll] *Bellarmyne* hauing set downe the former proposition, That God doth not incline a man to euill, eyther *Physicè vel Moraliter,* naturally or morally, he expoundeth what is vnderstood by ech of these termes, to witt, That Naturall or Phisicall concurrence is, when God concurreth to the substance of the action, as mouing or

impelling

The sume of Cardinall Bellarmynes discourse and Answere.

The second supposed contradictiō about *Moraliter.*

a *Bellar. de amiss. grat. & stat. pec-cat. l. 2. c. 13.*
b *Ibid. paulò post.*

impelling a mans will: but *Morall* concurrence is, when he doth commaund or ordayne any fynne to be done. As for example, If a great man fhould concurre to the murther of another, he may doe it in two manners, eyther Naturally or Phifically, concurring to the action it felf of poyfoning, ftrangling, or the like: or Morally, by counfelling or commaunding the fame to be done, which is properly called *Morall* concurrence. And by none of thefe two wayes, God doth concurre to the committing of a fynne.

Occafio-nall cō cur-rence to a finne what it is.

XLII. But there is a third way of concurring, tear-med *Occafionaliter*, occafionaly, or by giuing occafion, which improperly alfo may be called *Morall*: and this is, When God feeing an euill man euill-difpofed, to doe this or that fynne, though he doe not concurre therunto by any of the forefaid two wayes, of affifting or com-maunding the action to be done: yet doth he, by his diuine prouidence, and goodnes, make occafions fo to fall out, as this fynne, and not that, is committed; and confequently it may be faid, That almighty God, without any fault of his, or concurrence in any of the forfaid two wayes, hath bene the Occafionall caufe of

Gen. 37.

this fynne. As for example, we read in *Genefis*, That when the brethren of *Iofeph* were obftinately bent to kill him, God, by the paffing by of certayne *Ifmaelites*, Merchants of *Galaad*, gaue occafion of his felling into *Egypt*; fo as he was herby fome Occafionall, or Morall caufe of this leffer fynne, for efchewing the greater, but not in the former fenfe of Morall concurrence, which includeth alfo commandement.

XLIII. This Occafionall concurrence then, though in fome large fenfe, it may be called alfo *Morall*: yet is it much different from the former, and confe-quently, the one may be affirmed, and the other denyed, without any contradiction at all. And fo this fecond obferuation againft Cardinall *Bellarmyne*, is wholy impertinent

pertinent: for that *Contradictio* must be *in eodem, respectu eiusdem*, which heere is not verifyed. For that when the Cardinall saith in the first place, That God doth not côcurre Morally to synne, he meaneth by comâuding or counselling the same: & whê in the later place, he graûteth, That God doth côcurre somtymes Morally, he meaneth by giuing occasiô only for this synne to be cômitted, rather then that, which is a plaine different thing.

XLIIII. And of the same quality is the third Contradiction, et downe by the Apologer in these wordes : *All the Fathers teach constantly (saith Bellarmyne) that Bishops doe succeed the Apostles, and Priests the seauenty disciples.* And then in another part of his workes, he affirmeth the contrary: *That Bishops doe not properly succeed the Apostles.* But whosoeuer shall looke vpon the places here quoted, shall fynde this to be spoken in diuers senses, to witt, that they succeed them in power of Episcopall Order, and not in power of Iurisdiction, and other extraordinary priuiledges: so as both those doe well stand togeather. And the like I say of the 4. contradiction obiected, which is , *That Iudas did not belieue* : & yet in an other place, *That Iudas was iust, and certaynly good:* which is no contradiction at all, if we respect the two seuerall tymes, wherof Cardinall *Bellarmyne* doth speake, prouing first, out of *S. Iohns* Ghospell, by the interpretation of *S. Hierome*, that *Iudas* at the beginning was good, and did belieue; and then by other words of *Christ* in the same Euangelist, vttered a good while after the Apostles vocation, *That he was a dyuell, and belieued not.* And who but our Apologer, would found a côtradictiô against so learned a man as *Bellarmyne* is, vpon a manifest Equiuocation of tymes, wherby he may no lesse argue with *Bellarmyne* for calling *S. Paul* an Apostle and persecutour, and *Nicolaus* an elect of the holy Ghost, and yet an Heretick, for that the one was a Persecutour first, and then an Apostle, and the other first a chosen

N   Deacon

The third supposed contradictiô, about Bishops succeeding of the Apostles.
Bellarm. de Cler. lib. 1, *cap.* 14.
Lib. 4. *de Pôtif. c.* 25.

The 4. côtradiction about Iudas.
Lib. 1. *de Pontif. c.* 12.
Lib. 3. *de Iustif. cap.* 14.
Ioan. 6.

Deacon by the holy Ghoſt, and afterward an Hereticke, poſſeſſed by the diuell, as moſt do hould.

XLV. But I ſhould doe iniury (as before I ſaid) both vnto Cardinall *Bellarmyne* and my ſelf, if I ſhould goe about to anſwere theſe ſuppoſed contradictions at length. To the Cardinall, in preuenting him, that will doe it much better. Vnto my ſelf, in ſpending tyme in a needles labour, for ſo much as euery one of meane iudgemēt, that will but looke vpon the bookes, and places themſelues heere cyted, will diſcouer the weaknes of theſe obiections, and that they haue more will, then ability to diſgrace Cardinall *Bellarmyne*

XLVI. After the obiecting then of theſe deuiſed contradictions, our Apologer returneth againe to exagitate yet further the foreſaid ſaying of *Bellarmyne*, That neither his Maieſty, nor other King hath need to feare any daunger to his Royall Perſon, by acknowledging the Popes ſpirituall authority in his Kingdome, more then other Chriſtians, and Monarches haue done heretofore, or doe now in other Kingdomes round about him, who admitt the ſame Authority and haue done euen from the beginning of their Chriſtianity, without any ſuch dangers of murther incurred therby. Wherupon this Apologer maketh a large new excurſion, numbering vp a great Catalogue of contentions, that haue fallen out, betweene ſome Popes and Emperours, & the ſaid Emperours receaued hurtes, domages, and dangers therby, and conſequently had cauſe to feare, contrary to that which *Bellarmyne* writeth.

XLVII. And in this enumeration the Apologer bringeth in the example of the Emperour *Henry* the 4. brought to doe pennance at the Caſtle of *Canuſium*, by Pope Gregory the ſeauenth; as alſo of the Emperour *Fredericke* the firſt, forced by Pope *Alexander* the third *to lie agrooſe* (as his word is) *on his belly, and ſuffer the other to tread on his necke :* Of the Emperour *Philip*, that is ſaid

to

The Apologer returneth to calumniate Popes.

,,
,,
,,
,,

Examples obiected of Princes moleſted by Popes.

to haue bene slaine by *Otho* at the Popes motion; and
that in respect therof, the said *Otho* going to *Rome*, was
made Emperour, though afterward the Pope deposed
him also : Of the Emperour *Fredericke* the second, excommunicated, and depriued by Pope *Innocentius* the
fourth, who in *Apulia* corrupted one to giue him poyson, and this not taking effect, hyred one *Manfredus* to
poyson him, wherof he dyed : That Pope *Alexander* the
third wrote to the *Soldane* to murther the Emperour, &
sent him his picture to that effect : That Pope *Alexander*
the sixth, caused the brother of *Baiazetes* the Turkish
Emperour, named *Gemen*, to be poysoned at his brothers
request, and had two hundred thowsand crownes for
the same : That our King *Henry* the second, besides his
going barefooted in pilgrimage, was whipped vp and
downe the Chapter-howse, like a schoole-boy, and
glad to escape so too : That the Father of the moderne King
of *France*, was depriued by the Pope of the Kingdome of
Nauarre, and himself (I meane this King of *France*)
forced to begge so submissiuely the relaxation of his
excommunication, as he was content to suffer his Em-
bassadour to be whipped at *Rome* for pennance.

Apolog.
pag. 72. 73.
“
“
“
“
“
“
“
“
“
“
“
“
“
“
“
“
“

XLVIII. All these examples are heaped togeather
to make a muster of witnesses, for proofe of the dangers wherin Princes persons are, or may be, by
acknowledging the Popes Supreme Authority. But
first in perusing of these, I fynde such a heape indeed
of exaggerations, additions, wrestings, and other
vnsyncere dealings, as would require a particuler Booke
to refute them at large. And the very last here metioned
of the present King of *France*, may shew what credit is
to be giuen to all the rest, to witt, *That he suffered his Embas-*
sadour to be whipped at Rome, & the latin Interpreter turneth
it, *Vt Legatum suum Romæ virgis cæsum passus sit*: as though he
had bene scourged with rodds vpon the bare flesh, or
whipped vp and downe *Rome*; wheras so many hun-

N 2   dreds

dreds being yet aliue that faw that Ceremony (which was no more, but the laying on, or touching of the faid Embaffadours fhoulder with a long white wand vpon his apparell, in token of fubmitting himfelf to Ecclefiafticall difcipline) it maketh them both to wonder, and laugh at fuch monftrous affertions, comming out in print: and with the fame eftimation of punctuall fidelity doe they meafure other things here auouched.

I X L. As for exáple, that our King *Henry* the fecond *was whipped vp and downe the Chapter-houfe, & glad that he could efcape fo too*, for which he cyteth *Houeden*, and this he infinuateth to be, by order of the Pope: in refpect wherof (he faith) the King had iuft caufe to be afraid. But the Author doth plainly fhew the contrary, firft fetting downe the Charter of the Kings abfolution, where no fuch pennáce is appointed: & fecondly after that againe in relating the voluntary pennances which the King did at the Sepulcher of *S. Thomas*, for being fome occafió of his death, doth refute therby this narration, as fraudulent, and vnfyncere, that the King *was whipped like a fchool-boy by order of the Pope*, as though it had not come fró his owne free choice, and deuotion.

L. That other inftance of the Emperour, *that lay a-groofe on his belly* (which I fuppofe he meaneth of *Fredericke* the firft) and fuffered Pope *Alexander* the third to tread on his necke, is a great exaggeratió, and refuted, as fabulous, by many reafons, and authorityes of *Baronius*, to whome I remit me. The other in like máner of *Celeftinus* the Pope, that fhould with his foote beate of the Crown from the head of *Henry* the fixt Emperour, being only mentioned firft of all others by *Houeden* an Englifh Authour, and from him taken by *Ranulph* of *Chefter*, no other writer of other nations, eyther prefent at his Coronation as *Godefridus Viterbienfis* his Secretary, or others afterward as a *Platina*, b *Nauclerus*, c *Sabellicus*, d *Blondus*, e *Sigonius*, f *Crantzius*, fo much as mentioning the fame, though yet they

Touching K. Henry the fecód.

Houed. pa. 303.

Ibi. pa. 308.

See Baron. in an. 1177. fub finem.

a *In vita Celeftini*
b *part. 2. gen. 40. in anno 1190.*
c *Tom. 2. Ennead. li. 5*
d *in anno 1190.*
e *Lib. 15. in Henrico 6.*
f *Lib. 7. Saxon. cap. 3. & alij.*

they write of his Coronation, maketh it improbable, and no lesse incredible then the former.

LI. That also of the Emperour *Philip*, affirmed to be slaine by *Otho* his opposite Emperour, at the incitation of Pope *Innocentius* the third, is a meere slauder. For that, according to all histories, not *Otho* the Emperour, but an other *Otho* named of *VVitilispack* a priuate man & one of his owne Court, vpon a priuate grudge, did slay him. And albeit *Vrspergensis*, that followed the faction of the Emperours against the Popes, doe write, that he had heard related by some the speech here sett downe, that *Innocentius* should say, That he would take the Crowne from *Philip*, or *Philip* should take the Myter from him: yet he saith expresly, *Quod non erat credendum*, that it was not to be belieued. And yet is it cyted here, by our Apologer, as an vndoubted truth, vpon the onely authority of *Vrspergensis* in the margent.

LII. The like may be said of the tale of *Frederick* the second, attempted to haue bene poysoned, first in *Apulia* by Pope *Innocentius* the 4. and afterward effectuated by one *Manfredus*, as *hyred by the Pope*: which is a very tale in deede, and a malicious tale. For that he which shall read all the Authors that write of his life, or death, as [1] *Platina* (whome the Protestants hold for free in speaking euill of diuers Popes) [2] *Blondus*, [3] *Sabellicus*, [4] *Nauclerus*, [5] *Crantzius*, [6] *Sigonius*, & others, shall fynd, that as they write very wicked thinges committed by him in his life: so talking of his first danger in *Apulia* by greuous sicknes, they make for the most part no mention of poyson at all, and much lesse as procured by the Pope *Innocentius*, praysed * for a very holy man, and to haue proceded iustly against Fredericke. And secondly for his death, they agree all, that it was not by poyson, but by stopping his breath and stifelyng him in his bed with a pillow, by *Manfredus* his owne bastard Sonne, to whome he had giuen the Princedome of *Tarentum*, for feare least

N 3   he

Vrspergensis pag. 310. Sigonius li. 15. in fine c. 13. Crantzius in sua Saxonia li. 7. cap. 28. Nauclerus. part. 2. gen. 41. in An. 1208. idem Cuspinianus, Crusius & alij.

1 *In vita Innocětij 4.* 2 *Li. 2. Decad. lib. 7.* 3 *Tomo 2. Enne. 9. l. 6. non longè ante finem.* 4 *Parte 2. gen. 41. an. 1247.* 5 *Lib. 8. ca. 18. suæ Saxoniæ.* 6 *In fine lib. 18.* * *Blond. vbi supra.*

he fhould take it from him againe, and beftow it vpon *Conradus* his other foone. But that the Pope was priuy to this, or hyred him to doe the fact, as our Apologer affirmeth; there is no one word or fillable in thefe Authors therof.

LIII. But you will fay, that he cyteth one *Petrus de Vineis* in his margent, and *Cufpinian* in the life of *Fredericke*, both which are but one Authour; for that *Cufpinian* profeffeth to take what he faith, out of *Petrus de Vineis*, which *Petrus* was a feruant to *Fredericke*, and a profeffed enemy to the Pope, and wrote fo partially of this contention, as Pope *Innocentius* himfelf wrote *Libros Apologeticos* (as *Blondus* recordeth) Apologeticall Bookes to confute the lyes of this *Petrus de Vineis* in his liue tyme: And yet yow muft note, that he auoucheth not all that our Apologer doth, nor with fo much ftomacke, or affirmatiue affertion. For thus relateth *Cufpinian* the matter, out of *Petrus de Vineis*: *Non potuit cauere, &c.* The

Petrus de Vineis lib. 2. epift. 2. & Cufp. in Vita Frederici 2.

Blondus Ibid.

” Emperour could not auoyd, but when he returned
” into *Apulia* he perifhed with poyfon, the 37. yeare of his
” raigne, and 57. of his age, on the very fame day that he
” was made Emperour. For wheras at the towne of
” *Florenzola* in *Apulia*, hauing receaued poyfon he was dan-
” geroufly ficke, and at length, by diligence of Phifitions,
” had ouercome the fame, he was ftifeled by *Manfredus*
” his baftard fonne, begotten of a noble woman his
” Concubine, with a pillow thruft into his mouth, whe-
” ther it were, that *Manfredus* did it, as corrupted by his
” enemyes, or by the Pope, or for that he did afpire to the
” Kingdome of *Sicilia*. So he.

LIV. And albeit, as yow fee, he faith more herin againft the Pope, then any of the other Authours before mentioned, for that he defired to caft fome fufpitions vpon him : yet doth he it not with that bold affeueration, that our Apologer doth, faying : *That both his firft ficknes was by poyfon, of the Popes procurement, and his mur-*
thering

Inforcing of matters againft the Pope.

thering afterward by hyring of Manfredus *to poyson him againe :* whereas the other ascribeth not the first poysoning to the Pope (if he were poysoned) neyther doth so much as mention the second poyson, but onely the stifeling, and finally leaueth it doubtfull, whether the same proceeded from the Emperours enemyes, or from the Pope, or from his Sonnes owne ambition, and emulation against his brother.

LV. To the other obiection, or rather calumniation out of *Paulus Iouius,* that *Alexander* the third did write to the *Soldane,* That if he would liue quietly, he should procure the murther of the Emperour, sending him his picture to that end : It is answered, that no such thing is found in that second booke of *Iouius,* by him here cyted, nor elswhere in that History, so far as by some diligence vsed I can synde : and it is not likely, it should be found in him, for so much as he beginneth his History with matters only of our tyme, some hundreds of yeares after *Alexander* the third his death.

Apolog. pag. 73.

LVI. So as the only chiefe accusation, that may, seeme to haue some ground against any Pope, in this catalogue, for procuring the death of any Prince, is that which he alleadgeth out of *Cuspinian,* that *Alexander* the sixth tooke two hundred thowsand Crownes of *Baiazetes* Emperour of the Turkes, to cause his brother *Gemen* to be put to death, whome he held captiue at *Rome,* which he performed (saith our Apologer) by poyson, and had his pay ; this I say, hath most apparence : for that some other Authors also besides doe relate the same, affirming, That albeit Prince *Gemen* the Turke, when he dyed, eyther at *Caieta,* or *Naples,* or *Capua,* (for in this they differ) was not the Popes prisoner, but in the hands of *Charles* the 8. King of *France,* who tooke him from *Rome* with him, when he passed that way with his army : yet that the common fame or rumour was, that Pope *Alexander* the sixth, had part therin, or, as *Cuspinians* words

About the death of Gemen or Sizimus brother to the great Turke.

Lib.2.hiſt,

a *In vita
Alexand.
ſexti.*
b *Ennead.
10.lib.9.*

words are, *Pontifice non ignorante,* the Pope not vnwitting
therof. The reaſon of which report *Guicciardine* alleadgeth to be this, to wit, That the euill nature and condition of Pope *Alexander,* which was hatefull to all men,
made any iniquity to be belieued of him.ᵃ *Onuphrius Pan-
uinus* writeth that he dyed in *Capua* of a bloudy flux
without any mention of poyſon. And ᵇ *Sabellicus* before
him againe, relateth the matter doubtfully ſaying; *Fue-
runt qui crederent,eum veneno ſublatum,&c.* There were ſome
that belieued, that he was made away by poyſon, and
that *Alexander* the Pope was not ignorant therof; for that
he was ſo alienate in mynde from the French-men, that
he was loath they ſhould take any good by him : Thus
we ſee, that the matter is but doubtfully and ſuſpi-
ciouſly related only, and the French-men being angry
for his death, by whome they hoped great matters,
might eaſily brute abroad a falſe rumour, for their owne
defence in that behalfe.

LVII. But as for the two hundred thowſand
crownes, though *Iouius* doe ſay, that they were offered
by *Baiazet,* as alſo *Veſtis inconſutilis Chriſti,* The garment of
our Sauiour without ſeame : yet doth he not ſay, that
they were receaued, eyther the one, or the other. So as
whatſoeuer euill is mentioned of any Pope, our Apologer maketh it certayne: and when it is but little, he
will inlarge it to make it more : and when it is ſpoken
doubtfully, he will affirme it for a certaynty: wherin he
diſcouereth his owne humour againſt Popes, and therby
limiteth the Readers faith in belieuing him; though we
do not take vpon vs to defend the liues and facts of all
particuler Popes, but their faith and authority ; being
forewarned by our Sauiour, that vpon the Chayre of
Moyſes ſhall ſit Scribes and Phariſyes, whome we muſt
obey, in that they teach, and not follow or imitate, in
that they doe. And this ſhall ſerue for this point : Card.[11]
Bellarmyne, I doubt not, will be more large. If a man
would

would go about to difcredit Kingly authority, by all
the mifdeeds of particuler Kings that haue byn regiftred
by Hiftoriographers, fince the tyme that Popes began,
he fhould fynde, no doubt, aboundant matter, and fuch,
as could not be defended by any probability. And yet
doth this preiudicate nothing to Princely power or dignity, and much leffe in our cafe, where the facts themfelues obiected, are eyther exaggerated, increafed, wre-
fted, or altogeather falfifyed.

The third Part of this Paragraph.

HERE remayneth the laft part of
this impugnation of the Cardinalls
letter, which confifteth in the exa-
mining all the Authorityes and Sentences of ancient Fathers, alledged
by him in the fame. As firft of all, the
comparifon of the art, and deceipt
vfed by *Iulian* the Emperour, furnamed *Apoftata*, and
recounted by *S. Gregory Nazianzen*, in placing, and in-
ferting the images of his falfe Gods, into the pictures
of the Emperour, in his Imperiall banner: fo, as no man
could bow downe, or reuerence the Emperours picture,
(as then was the cuftome) but that he muft adore alfo
the images of the falfe Gods. Which art of temperament,
the Cardinall doth compare vnto this mixture & com-
bination of claufes lawfull, and vnlawfull, Cyuill, and
Ecclefiafticall in the *Oath* propofed; fo as a man can
not fweare the one, but he muft fweare alfo the other.

O   Which

1.
Apolog.
pag. 78.

*Nazian.
orat. 1. in
Iulian.*

The exam-
ple of Iu-
lians bâner
examined.

Which fimilitude, although it do expreffe moft fitly the matter in hand; yet the Apologer being forely preffed therwith feeketh many euafions to euacuate the fame, by fearching out diffimilitudes, and faying; That albeit a fimilitude may be admitted *claudicare vna pede*, to limp, or halt on one foote: yet this (faith he) *is lame, both of feete & hands, and euery member of the body*: And then he taketh vpon him to fet downe at length the diuerfityes that may be picked out. As firft, that *Iulian* was an *Apoftata*, ,, but our Soueraigne is a Chriftian: he changed the Reli- ,, gion which he once profeffed, but our King not: he ,, became an Ethnicke, or an Atheift, our King is not ,, afhamed of his profeffion : *Iulian* dealt againft Chri- ,, ftians, but his Ma.ᵗⁱᵉ dealeth only to make a diftin- ,, ction betweene true fubiects, and falfe-harted tray- ,, tours. And fo he goeth forward to weary his Reader with many more like diuerfityes, which muft needs be loathfome to euery man of meane iudgment, who know that a fimilitude requireth not parity in all poynts (for then it fhould be *idem*, and not *fimile*) but only in the poynt wherin the comparifon is made, as heere in the compounding and couching togeather of lawfull and vnlawfull things in the *Oath*, as the other did in his banner.

LIX. For if a man would tryfle, as our Apo- loger doth, and feeke out differences betweene things, that are compared togeather, as like in fome certayne

Similitu-
des hold
not in all.

poynts, but vnlike in other; we fhould ouerthrow all fimilitudes whatfoeuer, and confequently we fhould eneruate many moft heauenly fpeaches of our Saui- our in the Ghofpell , that ftand vpon fimilitudes.

Matth. 10.

As for example : *Be you wife as Serpents, and fimple as Doues.* What enemy of Chriftian Religion might not cauill, and calumniate this? feeking out diuerfityes betwixt a ferpent and a man, and betweene the malicious craft of that malignant creature, and the wifedome that

ought

ought to be in a prudent man. But it is sufficient that
the similitude do hold in that particuler poynt, wherin
Christ made the comparison. And so agayne, When our
Sauiour maketh the comparison betweene the Kingdome of heauen, and the litle grayne of mustard-seed;
who cannot fynd out infinite differences betweene the *Matth.13.*
one and the other, making the similitude to halt and *Mar. 4.*
limp in many more parts, then it can go vpright. But *Luc.13.*
it is sufficient, that it stand, and halt not in that one
poynt, wherin the comparison is made.

    LX. I passe ouer many other like similitudes, as *Ibid.*
that the Kingdome of heauen, is like to a man that sow-
eth good seed in his field: As also it is like to leauen,
which a woman tooke and hid in three measures of
meale, vntil the whole was leauened: It is like also to a
treasure hid in the ground; and to a Marchant man,
that seeketh good margarites, and precious stones: And
vnto a net cast into the sea, and gathering togeather
of all kynd of fishes. Who cannot (I say) fynd out differences and diuersityes, if he would study for them in all
these similitudes vsed by our Sauiour. For as for the
last of the net, that gathereth togeather perforce, good
and bad fish in the sea, seemeth hard to be applyed to
the Kingdome of heauen, whether we vnderstand it,
eyther of Gods Kingdome in the next world, or of the
Church in this; for that in the next world good & bad
are not admitted; and in this world, the Church of
Christ gathereth none perforce, as the net doth. But yet
in the poynt it selfe, wherin Christ our Sauiour made
the comparison, the similitude doth hold; and that is
sufficient to shew the impertinent indeauour of this A-
pologer heere, to seeke out diuersityes, that appertayne
not to the poynt wherin the comparison is made.

    LXI. The next example which our Apologer see-
keth to auoyd or euacuate in the Cardinalls letter, is
that of old *Eleazar* in the booke of *Machabees,* who rather

    then

2. Mach. 6.

About the
example of
Eleazar.

Apol. pag.
81.

        ,,
        ,,
        ,,
        ,,

then he would do a thing vnlawfull, and againſt his owne conſcience, or that might be ſcandalous to others, he refuſed not to ſuffer all kynd of torments ; which the Cardinall applyeth to the taking of this vnlawfull *Oath*, by ſuch as are Catholicks, but eſpecially by the *Arch-prieſt*, head of the Clergie in *England*, whoſe caſe he preſumeth to be more like to that of *Eleazar*, for his age, eſtimation, and authority aboue the reſt. To which example the Apologer anſwereth thus : That if the Arch-prieſts ground of refuſing this *Oath* were as good as *Eleazars* was, for refuſing to eate of the ſwynes-fleſh that was propoſed, and vrged vnto him, it might not vnfitly be applyed to his purpoſe : *But the ground ſayling,* (ſaith he) *the building cannot ſtand.* But this is an eſcape much like the former, that runneth quite from the matter : for that the Cardinall ſuppoſeth a Catholicke conſcience in him to whome he writeth, to which conſcience it is as repugnant to ſweare any thing, ſounding againſt any poynt of Catholicke Religion or Doɛtrine, as it was to *Eleazar* to eate ſwynes-fleſh, againſt the law of *Moyſes.* Which ſuppoſition being made, and that in the Cardinalls iudgment, this *Oath* conteyneth diuers clauſes preiudiciall to ſome poynts of the ſaid Catholicke beliefe and doɛtrine concerning the authority of the Sea Apoſtolicke, and that the taking therof would not only be hurtfull to the taker, but offenſiue alſo, and ſcandalous to many other of that Religion, both at home and abroad ; the application of this example of *Eleazar* was moſt fit and effeɛtuall. Let vs ſee what enſueth of the reſt of the Authorityes.

    LXII. The third example is of *S. Baſill* ſurnamed for his rare learning and holineſſe, *The great,* who being moſt earneſtly exhorted (as *Theodoret* recounteth the ſtory) by *Modeſtus* the deputy of *Valens* the *Arrian* Emperour, ſent of purpoſe to that effeɛt, that he ſhould accōmodate himſelf to the ſaid Emperours will, & preſent

3.

Apol. pag.
84.

*Theodoret
lib. 4. c. 19.*

sent tyme, and not suffer so many great Churches to be abandoned (for that all such bishops, as would not accommodate themselues were sent into banishment) for a little needles subtility of doctrines, not so much to be esteemed: offering him also, the friendship of the Emperour, and many other great benefits to ensue, both to him and others, if he would in this poynt shew himselfe conformable. But this holy and prudent man (saith the Cardinall)answered, That it was not to be indured, that any one syllable of * dyuine doctrynes, should be corrupted, or neglected; but rather, that for the defence therof, all kynd of torment was to be imbraced. Out of which example the Cardinall doth gather, how strict and wary a good man must be, in yealding to any thing neuer so litle, that is preiudicall to the integrity of Catholicke doctryne: and it seemeth very fit to the purpose, and the cases somwhat like.

The tentation of S. Basil by theDeputy Modestus.

* Diuinorū dogmatum.

LXIII. Yet doth our Apploger by all meanes possible seeke to wype of, or weaken all that can be inferred out of this example. And first of all, he beginneth with a meere calumniation thus: First I must obserue (saith he) that if the Cardinall would leaue a common and ordinary tricke of his, in all citations, which is, to take what makes for him, and leaue out what makes against him, & would cyte the Authors sense, as well as the sentence; we should not be so much troubled with answering the Ancients which he alledgeth. And to instance it in this very place, if he had continued his allegation but one lyne further; he should haue found this place of *Theodoret*, of more force, to haue moued *Blackwell* to take the *Oath*, then to haue dissuaded him from it. For in the very next words it followeth (in *S. Basils* speach:) I do esteeme greatly the Emperours friendship, if it be ioyned with piety, but without it, I hold it for pernicious. So he.

Pag. 84.

A cauill against Belarmyne.
“
“
“
“
“
“
“
“
“
“
“
“

LXIV. And do these words last adioyned make

O 3   any

any thing at all for our Apologer ? Or rather agree they not fitly to the purpose of the Cardinals exhortation, though for breuityes sake he left them out ? How then is their omission brought in for a profe of *A common & ordinarie tricke of the Cardinals , in all his citations, to take only that which is for him, & leaue out what makes against him ?* How is this against him ? Or how doth this shew any such *ordinary tricke* of falshood in the Cardinal, not in one or two, but in all his citations? Doth this man care what he saith ? This then is one shift, to answere this *Ancient,* or rather *Anticke,* as heere he is made. Let vs see an other.

LXV. His second is by taking aduantage of translation out of the Greeke, in which *Theodoret* wrote his story, or rather by peruerting the same in some pointes to his purpose. For which cause he repeateth againe the substance of the history in these wordes : But that it may appeare (saith he) whether of vs hath greater right to this place (of *Theodoret* about *S. Basil*) I will in few wordes shew the Authous drift. The Emperour *Valens* being an *Arrian,* at the perswasion of his wife, whe he had depriued all the Churches of their Pastours, came to *Cæsarea,* where S.*Basil was then Bishop ; who, as the story reporteth, was the light of the world. Before he came, he sent his Deputy to worke it, that *S. Basil* should hold fellowship with *Eudoxius* (which *Eudoxius* was Bishop of *Constantinople* and the principall of the *Arrian* faction) or if he would not, that he should put him to banishment. Now when the Emperours Deputy came to *Cæsarea,* he sent for *Basil,* intreated him honorably, spake pleasingly vnto him, desired he would giue way to the tyme , neyther that he would hazard the good of so many Churches *tenui exquisitione dogmatis,* promised him the Emperours fauour, and him elfe to be Mediatour for his good. But *S. Basil* answered, *These intising speaches were fit to be vsed to children, that vse to gape after*

fuch

Another shift a-gainst S. Basils te-stimony.

Aplo.Pag. 84. & 85.

* *Theodo-ret lib. 4. cap. 19. græcè. la-tinè cap.17.*

Compare this to our tymes.

such things. But for them that were throughly instructed in Gods word, they could neuer suffer any syllable therof to be corrupted. Nay, if need required, they would for the maintenance therof, refuse no kind of death. In deed the loue of the Emperour ought to be greatly esteemed with Piety; but Piety taken away, it was pernicious.

LXVI. This is the truth of the storie (saith he:) & I haue layd downe at length his declaration, to the end that his sleightes may the better appeare in eluding the force of this Answere of S. *Basil*, as though he had said only, *that no syllable of Gods word was to be suffered to be corrupted*, wheras his meaning was, not only of Gods word, or of Scriptures alone, but, *Ne vnam quidem syllabam diuinorum dogmatum*, not any one syllable of dyuine doctrine, taught by the Catholicke Church, and so much import his wordes in greeke, which are guylfully heere translated: for that insteed of the forealleadged sentence, wherein consisteth the substance of the said answere, to witt: *That for them that are throughly instructed in Gods word, they can neuer suffer any syllable thereof to be corrupted*, he should haue said: *That they that haue beene brought vp & nourished in sacred learning, cannot suffer any one syllable of dyuine doctrynes (of the Church) to be violated*, which is conforme also to S. *Basils* purpose in hand. For that the controuersy, which he and other Catholicke Bishops had with the *Arrian* Doctors in those dayes, was not only, nor immediatly about the Scriptures out of which the *Arrians* alleadged more aboundantly then their aduersaries, but about certayne doctrynes determined by the Church, especially by the Councell of *Nice, as namely* about the vse of the wordes and doctrines of *homusion*, or consubstantiality, *hypostasis*, substance, person, trinitie, and other the like; and whether they should say *Gloria Patri et Filio*, or *Gloria Patri cum Filio*; or *in Filio*, & such other differences, which vnto the Deputy *Modestus*, seemed but small matters and subtilityes of doctrine, but to S. *Basil* matters of great moment

Crafty conueiace in tranſlating.

οἱ δὲ ἴοῖς θεῖ-
οις λόγοις
ἐντεθραμμέ-
νοις, προσι-
μένη θείων
δογμάτων
ἐδὲ μίαν
ἀνέχον]
συλλαβήν.

moment: for fo much as they were now determined by the Church, and thereby made *Diuina dogmata*, Diuyne doctrines, though they were not all exprefly found in Scriptures. So as this fleight in tráflating *S. Bafils* anfwer, *That fuch as were throughly inftructed in Gods worde could neuer fuffer any fyllable therof to be corrupted* (as though he had meant only of Scripturs) is not fincere, neyther agreable eyther vnto the letter of the Greeke text, or meaning of *S. Bafill.*

The third fhift.

LXVII. Let vs fee then his third fhift, to put of this matter, which is the fame that before we haue mentioned in the firft example of *Iulian*, to witt, by feeking out differences, & difparityes, betweene the claufes or members that are compared togeather, faying: *That albeit* Bafil *and the* Arch-prieft *may haue fome comparifon; yet not our Orthodoxe King with an* Arrian *Emperour.* Bafil *was follicited to become an* Arrian : *but the Arch-prieft, not once touched for any article of faith.* And fo he goeth forward with many contrapofitions . But I haue fpoken fufficiently before of the weaknes of this manner of argument . And if we remoue the mentions of fome perfons, that may be offenfiue , the matters themfelues will eafily difcouer their conformity. For if yow had demaunded *Modeftus* the Deputy then , in fauour of what religion would he haue *S. Bafil* to conforme himfelfe & fubfcribe; he would haue faid the *Orthodoxe*, no leffe then the Iudges of *England* do now , that require this *Oath* :

Wherein the comparifon of S. Bafil and Modeftus may be like in our dayes.

And yet did not *S. Bafil* thinke fo. And if any man fhould haue called that Emperour an *Arrian*, it would haue bene no leffe offenfiue, then to call a Proteftant-Prince at his day, a *Caluinift* or *Lutheran* ; notwithftanding that the reafon of difference betweene the Catholicks and *Arrians* at that day, be the fame, that is betweene Catholicks and Proteftants at this day : to witt, the following, or impugning of the vniuerfall knowne Church , defcending from Chriftes tyme, vnto

Saint

Saint Bafils, and from *Saint Bafils* to ours.

LXVIII. There remayne yet 3. or 4. other exāples mentioned by the Cardinall in his Epiſtle to the *Archprieſt*, wherof the firſt two are of *S.Peter*, and *Marcellinus* the Pope, whoſe fortitude and diligence in ryſing agayne, he deſyreth him to imitate, if perhaps he followed their infirmity in falling. The other two, are of *S.Gregorie*, and *S. Leo*, two holy and learned Popes, and for that cauſe both of them ſurnamed the *Great*, who do ſet downe in dyuers places, the obligation that all Catholicke Chriſtian men haue, to hold vnion and ſubordination with the Sea Apoſtolicke. Vnto the firſt two examples, as there is litle ſaid, but diſparityes only ſought out, betweene *Peter* and *Marcellinus*, and the ſtory alſo of *Marcellinus* called in queſtion; ſo I leaue the ſame to the *Cardinall* himſelfe to treate more at large: for ſo much, as in his former books, & workes, he hath handled the ſame ſufficiently; as alſo the third obiection, made againſt S. *Gregorie*, about refuſing the name of *Vniuerſall Biſhop*. And the ſame I muſt ſay of the 4. alſo, S.*Leo*, whome the Apologer confeſſeth to be truly alledged againſt him, for exalting the Authority of S. *Peter*, and firmitie of his faith, which he putteth of with this ſcoffe borrowed from D.*Iohn Reynolds his booke of Conference in the Tower*, That as *Tully* ſaid to *Hortenſius* the *Orator*, when he praiſed immoderatly eloquence, *That he would lift her vp to heauē, that himſelfe might go vp with her* : ſo would S.*Leo* lift vp *S. Peter* with prayſes to the sky, that he being his heire, might go vp alſo, and be exalted with him.

LXIX. And after this ſcorne, he picketh out diuers ſentences of S.*Leo* his works, which ſeeme ſomewhat odious, & to contayne ouermuch praiſe, & exaltation of S.*Peter*, & his Authority; all takē out of the ſaid *Reynolds* Booke, as *Reynoldes* himſelfe had takē the greateſt part of thē out of M. *Iewell*, to whome the ſame was very ſuffi-

Three or 4. exāples togeather.

Apol. pag. 94.

Reynoldes Cōſerence. ca.1.diuiſ.2. *Cicero in Horten.*

The Apologers impugnation of S.Leo.

P   ciently

ciently anfwered before by D.*Harding*, and the moft of
them fhewed to be meere calumniations. The firft and
chiefe wherof is this, *That our Lord did take S.Peter into the
fellowship of indiuifible vnity*; which S. *Leo* his aduerfaries
going about to wreft to an abfurd fenfe, to wit, that
this *indiuifible vnity* muft eyther be in perfon,or nature
with Chrift, D. *Harding* fheweth playnly by *S.Leo* his
owne words,fenfe, and drift, that he meant it only of
the *indiuifible vnity* or fellowfhip of the high name *of Rocke
of the Church*, which Chrift our Sauiour the chiefe and
fundamentall *Rocke* imparted to none, but to S. *Peter*, and
confequently that vnity of name of *Rocke* was indiuifible
betwene them : which if eyther M.*Iewell*, or M.*Reynolds*,
or our Apologer would haue equally confidered, they
needed not to go about to difgrace fo ancient a Father
with fo meere a cauill: or at leaftwife it being once anfwered,they ought not to haue fo ofte repeated it againe,
without fome new matter, or reafon for the fame, or
impugnation of the former anfwere.

LXX. But I will not trouble yow with any
more at this tyme, albeit there enfue in the Apology
diuers other poynts that might be ftood vpon, not for
that they conteyne any great fubftance of matter, but
for that they feeme to proceed out of no fmall auerfion
of mynd, acerbity, and gall in the writer, againft all
fortes of Catholicke people : which Christ Iesvs
amend and mollify, and giue him light from heauen to
fee the truth, that he fo bitterly impugneth.

LXXI. And as he dealeth with S.*Leo*,fo doth he much
more in the fame kynd with D.ᵒʳ *Sanders*, and *Cardinall
Bellarmine*, cyting out of their workes, dyuers fentences
culled and layd togeather, that feeme leffe refpeétiue to
the Authority of temporall Kings and Princes, and all
this to incite more his Ma.ᵗⁱᵉ againft them, and thofe
of their Religion : and fynally,againft the *Cardinall*,he
concludeth in thefe wordes: *That God is no more contrary to*
                                                        Belial

Belial, light to darknes, and heauen to hell, then *Bellarmines estimation of Kings is to Gods.* Which is a very passionate Conclusion, if yow consider it well, for that setting asyde the preheminēce for iudging in matters of Religion, which in his Controuersyes he proueth both by Scripture, and testimony of all antiquity, to appertayne to Bishops and not to Princes (& so was practised for 300. yeares after Christ, when few, or no Kings, or Emperours were yet Christians;) in all other poyntes he speaketh so reuerently of them, and defendeth their Supreme Authority with as great respect as any Authour (perhaps) hath euer done before him. And to pretermit other places, let the Reader but looke ouer the first 16. Chapters of his Booke *de Laicis,* and he shall fynd not only the Authority of Princes proued to be from God, by many Scriptures, Fathers, Councels, Reasons, and other Authorityes of Saints, against *Anabaptists, Atheists,* and other miscreants of our tyme; but the quality also, and excellent power of the said Princely Authority so exalted both for making of lawes, iudging, condemning, waging warre, and like actions of supreme power; as will easily refute this cauillation.

LXXII. And among other propositions tending to that effect, he hath this in the beginning of his eleuenth Chapter, which he proueth largely, and of purpose throughout the same; not only, That Temporall Princes are to be obeyed out of Conscience, or for Conscience sake; but also, *Quod lex Ciuilis non minùs obligat in Conscientia, quàm lex Diuina* : That the Cyuil law of the Temporall Prince doth no lesse bynd the Subiect in Conscience, thē the law that commeth immediatly from God himself. And how then is Cardinall *Bellarmyne* said heere to be no lesse contrary to God, concerning Kings Authority, *then light to darknes, and heauen to hell?* But especially if yow consider further, that when Cardinall *Bellarmyne* in that booke, commeth to treat of the Authority of Tem-

porall

Aplo. Pag. 110.

Lib. de Laicis cap. 11.

Card. Bellarm. exalteth much Princely authority.

porall Princes in matter of Religion, though he set
downe this Conclusion, That, *Non pertinet ad eos Iudicium
de Religione*, The authority of iudging of Religion (which
is true or false) belongeth not vnto them, but vnto Bishops: yet, *Pertinet ad eos defensio Religionis*, the defence and
protection of Religion appertayneth vnto them: as also
the cyuill gouernmet in cyuill matters ouer all persons,
as well Ecclesiasticall as Temporall, which is so much as
a Catholicke man can giue to *Cæsar*, reseruing to *God*
that which is Gods.

LXXIII. And albeit this might be sufficiet to shew
the tooth that is held against Cardinall *Bellarmine*, and
the ardent appetite these Ministers haue to disgrace him
in somewhat: yet am I inforced to lay forth some few
examples more, wherby, as in a cleere glasse, the indifferent Reader will see, behold, and wonder also, at the
manner of dealing vsed against him to that end.

LXXIV. And now we haue already seene, what
general Conclusions haue bene gathered against him:
*That he vseth to contradict himselfe wittingly, so often as euer he is
pressed with any hard argument by his Aduersary: That his common
tricke is to tell the sentence of his Authour without his sense: That
he seeketh euery-where to debase Kingly authority, and the like.*
Which generalityes, as, in truth and reason, they may
not be inferred, but vpon proofe, and induction of
many particularyties: so when it commeth to tryall,
yow haue seene not so much, as any one particuler
sufficiently proued. Now shall yow heare some more
examples of calumnious dealing with him.

LXXV. Pag. 92. the Apologer speaking of *S.
Gregorie* the *Great*, and going about to interpret those
wordes of his, alleadged by the Cardinall, where he
calleth the Sea Apostolicke *Caput fidei*, the Head of faith,
in regard of the direction in matters of Faith, that is
to be taken from thence, as from the Head; the *Apologer*
would haue it vnderstood, that for so much as in that
place

Calûnious
dealing a-
gainst Car.
Bellar.

Greg. li. 11.
epist. 42.

place he speaketh to the Bishop of *Palermo* about the vse
of the *Pall*, accustomed to be gyuen by the sea Apostolicke
to Archbishops, *S. Gregories* meaning is, that the Sea
Apostolicke of *Rome* is head only in matters of Cerimo-
nyes, and then he inferreth thus: *VVhich sense* (saith he)
if yow will not admit, gine me leaue to say that once of one (Gregorie) *which Bellarmyne himselfe saith often of many of the Fa-*
thers, Minùs cautè locutus est : *Gregorie* spake not so aduisedly:
And the latin translation hath, *Quod ille de multis, & sæpè*
dicit, ex omni numero Patrū, That *Bellarmyne* saith it often, &
of many, and of all sortes of Fathers; to wit, that they
spake inconsideratly: and yet when I went to examyne
the two places of *Bellarmynes* workes, cyted by our Apologer in the margent, I found a strange abuse, to wit,
no such thing at all spoken of the Fathers, but only of
one *Nicolaus de Lyra,* made a Christian of a Iew, not much
aboue two hundred yeares past, who seeming by some
words of his, to hold a certayne extrauagāt opiniō, that
S. Peter, & *S. Paul* were not put to death at *Rome,* but at
Hierusalem, against the generall consent of all antiquity,
Cardinal *Bellarmyne* expoundeth first, what his true
meaning was, to witt, nothing in deed differing from
the Fathers expositions, and namely of *S. Hierome,* and
then addeth, *Quanquam minùs cautè locutus est &c:* Albeit
Lyranus in his manner of speach, was not so wary, as
he might haue byn, in giuing suspicion of so absurd an
opinion, and so contrary to all the ancient Fathers.
Heere then yow see, how matters are strayned. That
which *Cardinall Bellarmyne* speaketh only of *Nicolaus Lyranus*
vpon so iust occasion, as this was, is extended by our
Apologer, *to often, many, and all sortes of Fathers.* Is this good
dealing? How can the Apologer defend himself in this
place, from willfull exaggeration, and voluntary mistaking? In the other place cyted by him *lib. 2. de Christo*
cap. 2. there is no such matter at all. But let vs see some
other like examples.

Bellar. 2. de
Ro. Pontif.
cap. 10. &
li. 2. de Chri-
sto cap. 2.

Lyr. com. in
24. Matth.

LXXVI. Pag. 108. he setteth downe this generall
odious proposition out of *Bellarmyne* : *That Kings are rather*
slaues, then Lordes. And may a man thinke this to be true or
likely, that so rude a proposition should come from *Bel-*
larmine? Looke vpon the place by him cyted *lib. 3. de Laicis*
cap. 7. & yow will maruaile extremly at this manner of
proceeding. For that in this very place, yow shall fynd
that the *Cardinall* doth most exalt , and confirme by
Scriptures, Fathers, and other arguments, the dignity
and authority of the cyuill Magistrate among Christians. And in the next precedent Chapter before this
,, cyted, he hath this begining. The fourth reason, saith
,, he (to proue the lawfulnes and dignity of the Cyuill
,, Magistrate against the Anabaptists)is from the efficiēt
,, cause, to witt, God the Authour therof, from whom it is
,, certayne, that Cyuill power proceedeth , as S. Augu-
,, stine proueth throughout his whole fourth, and fifth
Prouer.8. books *De Ciuitate Dei,* and it is euident by the Scriptures,
,, for that God saith : *By me Kings do raigne &c.*
    LXXVII. So Bellarmine: and then passing to
the next Chapter heere cyted, which is the seuenth, he
proueth the same by another argument, which is. That
in the state of Innocency, if *Adam* had not synned, wee
should haue had Cyuil subiection and gouernment; and
consequently it cānot be thought to be euill, or brought
in by sinne, or for the punnishment of synne, as the *Ana-*
baptistes affirmed, but must needs be of God, & from God.
True it is (saith he) *that seruile, or slauish subiection, was brought*
in after the fall of Adam, and should not haue byn in the state of In-
nocency, but cyuill subiection should. And then he sheweth the
differences betweene these two sortes of gouernment,
and subiections, to witt, that the one, which is the seruile, tendeth wholy to the vtility and emolument of
him that gouerneth, and nothing to them that are gouerned. But the other which is cyuill and politick, tendeth principally to the profit of them that are gouerned

ned therby. *So as if there be any seruitude,* faith *Bellarmine* (but he meaneth not flauifh) *in this Ciuill principality, it falleth rather vpon him, that gouerneth the people to their owne vtility, then vpon the fubiectes that receaue the faid vtility therby.* And fo are Bifhops called the feruantes of their flockes, and the Pope himfelfe, *The Seruant of feruants* : and *S. Auguftine* vpon thofe wordes of our Sauiour in *S. Matthews* Ghofpell (*He that will be made firft* (or chiefe) *among you, muft be the feruant of all the reft*) doth proue at large, that, *In Ciuili Principatu, magis feruus eft, qui praeft, quàm qui fubeft* : In a Ciuill Principality, he is more a feruant that gouerneth to other mens profit, then he that obeyeth, to his owne.

Aug. li. 19. de ciuitate Dei cap. 14. Matth. 20.

LXXVIII. This is all that Cardinall *Bellarmyne* hath about this matter : wherin he doth fcarce name a King, as yow fee, but Bifhops, and Popes to be feruants in the gouermets of thofe, whome they gouerne; though he include good Kings in like manner, putting this difference betwene a good King, & a Tyrant, out of *Ariftotle* ; That a good king gouerneth to the profit of his Subiects, wherin he is their feruant in effect (though not their flaue, as this man odioufly vrgeth) and a Tyrant, that turneth all to his owne vtility without refpect of thofe, whome he gouerneth. And is this fo abfurd doctrine ? Or doth this iuftify the Apologers outragious propofition, *That Bellarmyne affirmeth Kings to be rather flaues then Lordes?* Who would not be afhamed of this intemperate accufation?

How good Kings and Princes are truly feruants.

Arift. li. 8. moral. c. 10.

LXXIX. And now there remayne eleuen places more of like quality, alleadged by the Apologer out of Cardinall *Bellarmynes* workes, which being examined by the Authors wordes, meaning, and fenfe, haue the fame want of fincerity which the precedent had. The fecond is, *That Kings are not only Subiects to Popes, to Bishops, to Priefts, but euen to Deacons.* This is a playne cauill : for the fault, if any be, falleth vpon *S. Chryfoftome,* and not vpon the Cardinall, whofe wordes are thefe : *S. Chryfoftome* in his

Apol. pag. 108. Libr. 1. de Pontif. c. 7.

his eyghtie and three Homilie vpon S. Matthewes ghospell, doth subiect Kings and Princes (in Eccle-siasticall matters) not only to Bishops, but also to Dea-cons. For thus he speaketh to his Deacon : *Si Dux quis-piam, si Consul, si is qui Diademate ornatur &c. If a Duke, if a Consul, if one that weareth a Crowne, commeth to the Sacramēt vn-worthily, restrayne him, and forbid him, for that thou hast greater power then he.* What fault hath Cardinall *Bellarmine* heere in alledging the words, and iudgement of *S. Chryso-stome?*

Libr. 1. de
Pont. c. 7.

LXXX. The third place is, *That an Emperour must content himself to drinke, not only after a Bishop, but after a Bishops Chaplin.* But these wordes are not found in *Bel-larmine*, but are odiously framed by the Apologer out of a fact of *S. Martyn* Bishop of *Towers* in *France,* related by

Sulpitius in
vita. D.
Martini.

auncient *Sulpitius* in his life, that he sitting one day at dynner with the Emperour *Maximus,* and the Empe-rours officer bringing a cup of wine to his Lord, he would not drinke therof first, but gaue it to the Bishop to beginne, who accepting therof, and drinking, deliue-red the said cup to his Priest to drinke next after him, thinking no lay-man to be preferred before a Priest, saith *Sulpitius.* But what doth this touch *Bellarmine,* that doth but relate the Story. May he, in truth, be said to auouch, that an Emperor must be cōtēt to drinke after a Bishops Chaplin? Who seeth not this violēt inforcemēt?

Ibid. & de
Cleric. c. 28.

LXXXI. His fourth place is this, *That Kinges haue not their Authority, nor office from God, nor his law; but from the law of Nations.* Good God! what desyre is here descried of calumniation? Let any man read the two places here quoted, and he will blesse himselfe, I thinke, to see such dealing. For in the first place his wordes are these: *Prin-cipatus secularis. &c. Secular Princedome is instituted by mā, & is of the law of Nations; but Ecclesiasticall Princedome is only from God, and by dyuine law,* which he meaneth expresly of the first institution of those Principalyties, or Gouernmentes:

for

for that at the beginning God did not immediatly appoynt these particuler and different formes of Temporall gouernment, which now the world hath, some of
Kinges, some of Dukes, some of Common-wealthes, but
appoynted only, that there should be Gouernment, leauing to ech nation to take or choose what they would.
But the Ecclesiasticall Gouernment by Bishops was or-
dayned immediatly by Christ himselfe, for which cause
Bellarmine saith in the second place heere alledged : *That*
Kingdomes are not immediatly instituted from God, but mediatly
only by meanes of the people; which people therfore
may change their formes of gouernment, as in many
Countryes we see that they haue : but yet when any
forme of Gouernment is established , and Gouernours
placed therin, their authority and power is from God,
and to be obeyed out of Conscience, vnder payne of
damnation, as before I haue shewed out of *Bellarmyne.*
And he that will read but from his third Chapter *de*
Laicis vnto the 13. shall fynd store of assertions & proofes
to that effect, to omitt many other places throughout
his workes. So as the former proposition, *That Kings haue*
not their Authority nor office from God nor his law , is very fraudulently sett downe. For if he vnderstand, that their
forme of Principality and Office therin, is not immediatly from Gods institution, but by meanes of humane
lawes, of succession, election, or the like; it is true. But
if he meane, that their Authority is not from God,
eyther mediate, or immediate, or induceth not obligation of Conscience in obeying them , as it seemeth he
would haue his Reader to thinke; it is most false. And
the Apologer ought not to haue walked in these obscu-
rityes, if he had meant vprightly.

    LXXXII. I am weary to wade any further in
these obiections, and yet will I not let passe to note
three more, though most briefly, and almost in three
words, leauing the rest to be examined by the Reader
himselfe. The first is, *That Church-men are as farre aboue*

           Q   *Kings*

*How Prin-
ces autho-
rity is me-
diatly or
imediatly
from God.*

Kings, _as the foule is aboue the body._ The other : _That Obedience due to the Pope, is for Confcience fake._ The third : _That Obedience due to Kings, is only for certayne refpeƈts of order and policy_ ; The firſt and laſt being meere calumniations and the other not denyed by vs. For as for the firſt, though the words heere mentioned be not in _Bellarmyne_ : yet the comparifon it felf of Ecclefiaſticall and Temporall powers in the Church, vnto the foule, and body, is the comparifon of

Naʒian. orat. ad Ci-ues timore perculſos & Imperat. iraſc.

S. Gregorie Naʒianʒen related only by _Bellarmyne_, and confequently it muſt needs follow, as the fame Father alfo inferreth, that fo much more eminent, as the foule is aboue the body, fo much more excellent is the power Ecclefiaſticall aboue Temporall, which _S. Chrifoſtome_ in like manner proueth at large in his books _de Sacerdotio_ : So as this is not Bellarmynes comparifon, but of the faid two auncient Fathers, and confequently _Bellarmyne_ is not here reprehended, but they.

L X X X I I I. The other two places, if they be two, and not one, but made two for multiplying of odious matter againſt vs, haue byn fo fully anfwered by vs before, as we ſhall need to fay no more heere therof. For as Obediéce is due out of Confcience vnto the Pope, & other Biſhops, & Spirituall Gouernours, in fpirituall

_Hebr._13.

Gouernments, by the Apoſtles precept, _Obedite Præpoſitis veſtris, &c._ Obey your Prelates, & be fubieƈt vnto them; for they watch, as being to render accompt for your foules : So the fame Apoſtle hath commanded alfo, due Obedience to Temporall Magiſtrates, in temporall affayres, by the fame obligation of Confcience, as Cardinall _Bellarmyne_ doth ſhew at large, in the places by me alledged. And I maruaile with what Confcience the Apologer heere can deny it, eyting a place for the fame in his margent, which hath no fuch matter, as he would

_Libr. de Cleric. c._28.

inferre, _That not for Confcience, but only for certayne refpeƈts &c._ For that treating of the obligation of Obedience to temporall lawes, in temporall affayres, his fecond propofition is; _Non funt exempti Clerici ab obedientia legum Ciui-lium_

lium: Clergie-men are not exempted from the obedience of temporall lawes. And in another place before cyted; *Lex Ciuilis non minùs obligat in conscientia quàm lex diuina*: The Temporall law byndeth no lesse in conscience, then the Diuine. So as all those odious matters are but frandulently layd togeather to make Catholicks, & their cause hatefull, especially vnto him, whom vnto they desyre most of all men vnder God, to yield most satisfaction for their temporall dutyes, and would hope also to effectuate it, if these make-bate Ministers did not by their continuall incitations, clamours, and false suggestions disturbe the same, and renew daylie iealosyes and distrustes in his Maties mynd against vs.

Libr. de Laicis c. 11.

The Conclusion.

WHERFORE to draw to an end of this distastfull argument, it cannot but grieue, & afflict much the hartes of all that loue eyther Prince or Countrey, & looke into the naturall sequels of like proceedings, to see matters runne dayly vnto such extremityes as they do, & that by such instigators, as are both both lesse carefull to foresee the hurts both priuate & publick that may ensue, & lesse able to remedy thē when they fall out. The principall of whom (being the first & chiefe motors) belydes the generall hatred wherin they are with both extremes of opposite in Religion, are so interessed in like máner by the spoyles, & rapines which their rauenous Purseuants daylie bring home, out of their continuall searches, and ransacks of innocent mens houses, goodes and persons, as litle moderation may be expected from them.

LXXXV. Would God it might please his dyuine Matie so to inlighten and illustrate that excellent vnderstanding of our Prince and Soueraigne, as he may see the many & great inconueniéces, that do & must follow vpon so violét courses as these men for their owne vti-litie

litie do fuggeſt, & profecute. Nothing can be more pittifull, then to fee a Noble Houfe diuided in it felfe,& the
one to beate,hunt,& purfue the other,& this to be their
continuall exercife , efpecially of Children, vnder the
fight of their owne Father, louing them all, and defy-
ring to be belou d. Ah! what follicitude muft there needs
be in that Fathers hart! And were it not a great fynne to
increafe the fame,by cafting in oyle to augmēt the flame?

　　L X X X V I.　Would God his Ma.ties eares,and thofe
of his wife Counfell could reach into thefe partes beyond the feas, and to all forrayne nations of Chriftendome befydes,to heare what is faid,what is writtē,what
is difcourfed by men of beft iudgment in this behalfe,
not only in regard of iuftice and piety, but in reafon
alfo of State and Policie ; no man being of fo fimple vn-
derftanding , but that he muft fee, that fo notorious dif-
ferēces,of Subiects for Religiō,purfued with fuch hofti-
lity among thēfelues, muft weaken greatly their forces,
and make them leffe efteemed both of friends and ad-
uerfaryes. So as, befydes internall dangers, which are
euer confequent vpon fuch inward diuifions,if forrayne
occafions fhould be offred vs agayne (as in former tymes
they haue beene) by forrayne warres; we fhould not
know how to truft the one the other.

　　L X X X V I I.　The cryes & cōplayntes of thefe afflictions running throughout Chriftendome, do giue
ftrange admiration vnto men, and do worke ftrong effectes both in iudgments and affections : Admiration,
for that no fuch thing was euer expected vnder his Maiefties gouernment , for many caufes : ftrong effectes,
for that they worke great alterations both in the one,
and the other : In iudgment,for that wife men fynd not
any reafon, eyther of Religion or State, why fuch extremityes fhould be purfued, with fuch rigour at the infti-
gation of partyes intereffed, to the euident danger of fo
great and honorable Kingdomes, who if in wills they
were vinted, as they are in one Prince and Gouernour;
their

their forces were both admirable and dreadfull: In affections, for that the compaſſion which naturally doth ac-
company our brethrens afflictions, eſpecially for a cauſe
that we moſt eſteeme and loue, to wit, our Religion;
muſt needes worke the contrary effect of inward auerſion, both in Princes & people abroad, notwithſtāding
they hold externall amity, and friendſhip for the tyme.

LXXXVIII. I let paſſe the generall obloquies, and
murmurations that are to be heard euery where, almoſt
in Chriſtendome, vpon this manner of proceeding, and
much more the publicke and priuate complaints, out-
cryes, and praiers that are made and offered daylie to
heauen, throughout all Catholicke Kingdomes lightly,
in all particuler Congregations, Oratoryes, Chappels,&
meetings of zealous men, that pray inſtantly to Almighty God for ſome remedy of theſe oppreſſions, and
perſecutions of Engliſh Catholicks, ſufficiently (as they
thinke) declared vnto thē & to the whole world by the
very printed Catalogues of Engliſh Statutes extant in
Print againſt them, for profeſſion of their Religion: for
that by the view of thoſe Statutes, they do eaſily con-
ceaue, what enormous effectes, do, and muſt follow in
the execution therof; albeit they did not both heare &
ſee daily ſo many lamētable preſidēts & ſpectacles therin.

LXXXIX. As for example, there haue not paſſed
many moneths, ſince there were ſeene ſome threeſcore
Prieſts more or leſſe (to omit others) caſt into baniſhmēt
about one tyme, & wandring vp and downe, throughout Chriſtēdome, according as euery man had occaſion,
or neceſſity for their mayntenance, gaue a lamentable
ſpectacle to all nations, to ſee mē of ſo good partes, amia-
ble aſpects, ſweet behauiour, naturall borne ſubiects of
the Lād, the moſt of them of very worſhipfull parētage,
all of learned education, cleere and deuoyd of any ſuſpi-
tion of crymes that could be obiected vnto them (for
otherwiſe they ſhould not haue bene diſmiſſed) in the
flower of their age, to be caſt out of their natiue ſoyle, for

profeſ-

professing that Religion only, wherby their said Countrey was first made Christian, & so continued vnder all
their noble Princes, Kings, Queenes, and Soueraignes,
Nobility, and Communatly, from the beginning of
their Conuersion, vnto this our age.

XC. This spectacle (I say) presented to the eyes of
most Nations of *Europe*, moued men not a litle, especially
hearing them protest their duetifull affections to his
Matie and Realme in all Cyuill & Temporall respects,
without seeking of any preferments, dignityes, riches, or
other emoluments by staying at home; but only the rest
& vse of their owne Consciences in matters of Religion,
which Protestāts in many other Catholicke Countryes
are suffered to inioy, though with farre lesser reason, in
regard of the ancient right & possession, which ech part
pretendeth for the vse of their said Religion.

XCI. And since this tyme agayne there hath beene
seene very lately another spectacle, not much vnlike to
the former (though much more markable) to wit, a like
number of Noble and Gentlemen, with their followers
and trayne, passing in very good sort through sundry
Countryes, being lately retyred out of his Maties Kingdome of *Irelād*, for the selfe same cause of their Consciēce,
and Religion; which when men do behold, and heare
them otherwise to speake honourably of his Matie &
the State, ascribing rather their afflictiōs to some vnder
Magistrates in *Ireland*, and Ministers that set them on; it
moueth more compassion, and maketh men thinke and
muse, what may be the end of all this, and whereunto
fynally it may grow? Whether the like may not be expected in tyme or doubted, out of other partes also of his
Maties dominions, vpon like angariatiō of Consciēces:
which points seeme to be of no small consideration, and
consequence to wise men; though those that be the immediate causes therof, will and must make light of all:
but the naturall yssue of such euentes, are not vnknowne.
And if the occasioners therof were guylty of no greater
                                                            fault

fault, but only to caſt his Matie & the State into perpetuall cares about the ſame (his Royall nature being in-
clined otherwiſe to ſweetnes, peace, and tranquillity) it
were a great ſynne in them, and ſcarce ſufferable.

XCII. Nor is the remedy heere attempted by our Mi-
niſter-Apologer (of denying all, and ſaying that there
is no perſecution, nor hard dealing with any, for matters of Religion, no not in the late Queenes dayes, when
ſo many were ſo rackt and rented for the ſame) any remedy at all; but rather a doubling of the iniury to the
afflicted, with encreaſe of exaſperation & auerſion of
myndes; as alſo a leeſing of all credit with others that
heare it, eyther at home or abroad : for that facts contrary to wordes, do preponderate with all ſober men,
and preuaile againſt the ſame.

XCIII. And truely, I cannot but wonder, why this
late Apology hath beene ſo greedily publiſhed by the
Apologer, both in Engliſh and Latyn to the world, for
that the Popes *Breues*, being but written priuatly to the
Catholicks of *England*, for informing their Conſciences
in a matter of neceſſary doctrine about the lawfulnes,
or vnlawfulnes of taking the *Oath*, and the Letter of
Cardinall Bellarmyne being directed only to a priuate
friend; both of them might haue remayned alſo pri-
nate, if this attempt had not byn made of publiſhing
the ſame. But now being drawne by the Apologer into
the Vniuerſall Theatre of the world, beſydes, that diuers will hold themſelues obliged, or at leaſtwyſe
prouoked to anſwere the ſame; it will follow alſo, that
the vnlawfulnes of the ſaid *Oath* to Catholicke Conſciences will more be ſeene, diſputed, & condemned by
all Vniuerſityes, Schooles, Bookes & Treatiſes of particuler learned men, throughout all Countryes of
Chriſtendome that profeſſe Catholicke Religiō. Wher-
vpon alſo the vniuſt violence, inforcing men to ſweare
the ſame *Oath*, vnder ſo rigorous paynes, as are the loſſe
both of goods & libertie, and therwithall to ſweare in

like

like manner , that they do it *willingly, freely, and without coaction* : will be cenſured (no doubt) for one of the greateſt contradictions in it ſelfe, and the moſt iniurious manner of proceeding with Chriſtian men, that euer, perhaps was heard of in the Chriſtian world.

XCIV. And this now occurred to me (deare Syr) to write to you côcerning my iudgmêt vpô this matter. What more may be ſaid to this Apologie, when it ſhall come into the handes of learned men; you will eaſily gheſſe by theſe few notes, that I haue heere laid togeather, which conteyne but little in reſpect of that which may be written of the matters heere handled . God of his endles mercy inclyne the hart of his Maieſty, to take the beſt way in this his courſe of Royall Gouernment : & for ſo much, as he hath byn pleaſed to ioyne ſo many Great Kingdomes vnder his only Scepter, and permitted them to haue ſo great differences of iudgements in matters of Religion, that their vnion of wills, at leaſt, in dutifull affections, may be ſo combined and conſerued by ſweet and temperate proceeding towards all , as deſpayre, the mother of headlong precipitation, enter not. The Prouerbe is knowne, *Qui nimium emungit, elicit ſanguinē : & patientia læſa vertitur in furorem.* I neuer heard or read, that too much violéce towards free Subiects euer ended well , eſpecially for ſuppoſed faultes that are not acknowledged for ſuch, by the puniſhed : & côſequently no hope of amendment by way of compulſion. Some may diſſemble for feare, but they are more loſt in their affections then the other . Some reaſonable toleration, and friendly treatie would bynd vp woundes from bleeding on all ſydes : Exulceration maketh them feſter more greiuouſly, and dangerouſly. To Gods holy Prouidence the whole is to be committed, who will diſpoſe of all to his greater glorie , *ſiuè in vitam, ſiue in mortem.* And to him alſo I committ yow, with my hartieſt Commendations, &c. This 10. of *Iune.* 1608.

F I N I S.